Researching Forensic Linguistics

Researching Forensic Linguistics is an informative, hands-on guide to conducting research in forensic linguistics that can underpin legal and justice practices and address social justice problems involving language.

Georgina Heydon takes readers step by step through the research process using case studies that draw on different types of forensic and legal language data such as police interviews, anonymous reports of sexual assault, threatening letters and justice stakeholder interviews. Each chapter is framed by a language problem arising from either forensic linguistic case work or a key issue in language and the law. Up-to-date research methods in forensic linguistics are presented, including authorship attribution using online corpora, practice-based linguistic analysis and experimental techniques.

This is an ideal companion for linguists who want to apply their skills to a forensic setting, practitioners in the legal and justice fields seeking to understand how linguistic analysis can support their work, and any student undertaking research in forensic linguistics within English language, linguistics, applied linguistics and legal studies.

Georgina Heydon is an Associate Professor of Criminology and Justice Studies at the Royal Melbourne Institute of Technology (Melbourne, Australia) and President of the International Association of Forensic Linguists.

Researching Forensic Linguistics
Approaches and Applications

Georgina Heydon

Routledge
Taylor & Francis Group
LONDON AND NEW YORK

First published 2019
by Routledge
2 Park Square, Milton Park, Abingdon, Oxon OX14 4RN

and by Routledge
52 Vanderbilt Avenue, New York, NY 10017

Routledge is an imprint of the Taylor & Francis Group, an informa business

© 2019 Georgina Heydon

The right of Georgina Heydon to be identified as author of this work has been asserted by her in accordance with sections 77 and 78 of the Copyright, Designs and Patents Act 1988.

All rights reserved. No part of this book may be reprinted or reproduced or utilised in any form or by any electronic, mechanical, or other means, now known or hereafter invented, including photocopying and recording, or in any information storage or retrieval system, without permission in writing from the publishers.

Trademark notice: Product or corporate names may be trademarks or registered trademarks, and are used only for identification and explanation without intent to infringe.

British Library Cataloguing-in-Publication Data
A catalogue record for this book is available from the British Library

Library of Congress Cataloging-in-Publication Data
A catalog record has been requested for this book

ISBN: 978-1-138-57598-1 (hbk)
ISBN: 978-1-138-57599-8 (pbk)
ISBN: 978-0-429-29064-0 (ebk)

Typeset in Goudy
by codeMantra

Printed and bound in Great Britain by
TJ International Ltd, Padstow, Cornwall

Contents

List of illustrations vii
Acknowledgements viii

Introduction 1

PART I
Language crimes 13

1 Authorship attribution case file: murder in Mackay 15
2 Legal language interpretation case file: solvency and semantics 29

PART II
Police procedures 39

3 Police interviewing: questioning strategies in UK and US models of training 41
4 Lie detection and linguistics 60
5 Police cautions and comprehension 78

PART III
Legal process 95

6 Anonymous reporting of sexual assault: assessing the value of online, form-based reporting 97
7 Legal investigative interviewing: questioning strategies in civil and administrative investigations 109

8	Access to justice: post-colonial language attitudes	126
9	Generating data for forensic linguistic research	139
	Index	153

Illustrations

Figures

1.1	Screenshot from the Birmingham Blog Corpus showing concordance results for *ather*	23
2.1	Diagram showing layers of analysis involved in a case to determine meaning in a legal text	35
4.1	SCAN courses in the United States 2018–2019 from http://www.lsiscan.com/id25_the_lsi_basic_course_on_scan.htm accessed 4 October 2018	64
7.1	Screenshot of questionnaire used with RCB group	115

Tables

1.1	Extract from the Mackay case data management spreadsheet showing ten lines of data	21
1.2	Final results of the data analysis for Mackay authorship attribution case	23

Excerpts

3.1	Extract from a police interview with a suspect (INT1) recorded in Victoria, Australia	44
3.2	Extract from a police interview with a suspect (INT2) recorded in Victoria, Australia	46
3.3	Extract from a police interviewing with a suspect (INT2) recorded in Victoria, Australia	46
3.4	Extract from a police interview with a suspect (INT1) recorded in Victoria, Australia	48
3.5	From Horvath et al. (2008: 107)	50
4.1	From www.lsiscan.com 'Can you find the confession in this statement?'	63
5.1	Caution given in INT4	80
5.2	Fingerprinting caution delivered in INT4	80
5.3	Fingerprinting caution delivery in INT8	84
5.4	Comprehension of fingerprinting caution delivered in INT1	85
5.5	Charging with criminal damage in INT1	86

Acknowledgements

All academic publications represent collaboration and dialogue between many people, only some of whose contributions are visible in the text. This book in particular draws on case studies and data sets I have analysed in the course of several such collaborative projects, some within the Forensic Linguistics and Interpreting Research Group at RMIT University, others within the Centre for Global Research and still others from further afield. I am grateful to my colleagues Jessica Findling, David Gilbert, Ceyhan Kurt, Miranda Lai, Eliseu Mabasso, Joe MacFarlane, Dian Dia-an Muniroh and Anastasia Powell for the opportunity of working with them and learning more about language and the law, and its related disciplines, than I could ever hope to have done on my own.

In addition, I have had the great benefit of feedback on the chapters in this book from a wide range of academic and professional colleagues, several of whom have contributed directly to this publication whilst others have assisted indirectly with feedback and advice over many years. In particular, I am grateful to Malcolm Coulthard, Diana Eades, Peter Gray, Alison Johnson, Roger Shuy and John Tedeschini for their generous and thoughtful advice. I hope that I have incorporated their suggestions appropriately, though any omissions or errors are my own.

As a serving member of the Executive Committee for the International Association of Forensic Linguists for eight years, I have the dubious distinction of having emailed almost every forensic linguist in the world at some time or other, chasing membership details or notifying members of system changes as we transitioned into the new world of online payments and web portals. Notwithstanding the humdrum nature of my communications with members, maintaining such a wide network of fellow forensic linguists has been crucial for the development of this book. I do not believe that I would have gained such insights into the key concerns of the field, nor understood the breadth of problems addressed under the banner of 'forensic linguistics' without the frequent interactions and scholarly exchanges I have enjoyed with colleagues around the world.

Naturally, this book would not exist without the editing and publishing support of the English Language, Linguistics, Translation and Interpreting studies team at Routledge. Special thanks to Louisa Semlyen, Hannah Rowe and Eleni Steck who at every stage exhibited a perfect balance of professionalism, sympathy and encouragement as required.

Finally, my family have always been supportive of my research career but I am especially indebted to my partner for his unwavering belief in my capabilities as a scholar and an author. To my child, now a teen, thank you for all the hugs, for tagging along to endless conferences and for not being *too* embarrassed when mum came to teach your English class about forensic authorship attribution.

Georgina Heydon
Melbourne, 2019

Introduction

In 2003, I was working as a part-time lecturer in linguistics at Monash University, Australia, when I had an almost Kafka-esque telephone conversation with an officer from the Attorney General's department in Canberra. Following a confusing opening sequence, during which I insisted I was not the person he thought I was, we eventually established that he really did want to talk to me and not to the full-time academic whose office I was occupying. It appeared that, against all probability, a bureaucrat somewhere in the federal government had read an article that I had written for the *Monash University Linguistics Papers*, a departmental journal with a print run of around 100 and no online presence (Heydon, 2002). With a justifiable sense of paranoia, I listened as the officer explained to me that his unit was interested in my research on a well-known, and (I believed) universally discredited, brand of lie detection called Scientific Content Analysis (Sapir, 1987; Smith, 2001; Vanderhallen, Vervaeke, & Mertens, 2008). He asked if I had reservations about the method. Perhaps undiplomatically, I said that I barely knew where to start. Indeed, I said, warming to my theme, the method was so obviously flawed that I hadn't actually been terribly interested in documenting what was wrong with it – I was more interested in understanding why any law enforcement agency would be tempted to use such twaddle in a criminal investigation. 'Ah,' he replied, 'well that's interesting because we use it when we vet our security staff for government offices.' He went on to explain that his team were unaware of any concerns about the method; it was taught by an apparently reputable private training agency in Australia and most likely they would continue to use it in their recruitment procedure.

The interaction has stuck with me all these years because it points to a failing in our approach to tackling language-based discrimination, injustice and poor practices in the legal system. To my mind, forensic linguists have not adequately considered how to overcome the fact that most legal professionals either don't know what a linguist does, or think that, because they use language for a living, they are themselves experts in the subject. Open any book on forensic linguistics and you will find in the introduction a detailed description of miscarriages of justice or other grave legal problems arising not only because of a language crime being committed but also because professionals and the general public have misconceptions about *how language works* (Coulthard, Johnson, & Wright, 2017; Eades, 1990;

2 *Introduction*

Gibbons, 1994; Oxburgh, 2016; Shuy, 1996; Solan, 1998). From the earliest published accounts of linguists applying systematic language analysis to address a legal problem (Svartvik, 1968), there is an underlying concern in the literature that the impact of the language problem is exacerbated by crude or misguided beliefs about language (Heydon, 2005b; Shuy, 1993). The linguistic problems themselves can be addressed with enough properly qualified researchers and adequate resources. We can identify best practice interpreting (Eva Nga Shan, 2015; Hale, Napier, Hale, & Napier, 2013; Hale, Roque, Spencer, & Napier, 2017; Licoppe & Verdier, 2013; Nakane, 2007, 2011; Napier & Spencer, 2017), we can suggest better questioning of witnesses (Conley & O'Barr, 2005; Johnson, 2008; Jol & van der Houwen, 2014), we can describe the points of conflict between police and suspects (Auburn, Drake, & Willig, 1995; Benneworth-Gray, 2014; Gibbons, 1996; Haworth, 2013; Heydon, 2005a, 2005c, 2012; Johnson, 2008; Linell & Jonsson, 1991), we can write better police cautions (Cotterill, 2000; Eastwood & Snook, 2012; Gibbons, 1990; Heydon, 2013; Nakane, 2007; Rock, 2007), we can recommend best practice for courtroom examination of vulnerable witnesses (Cooke, 1996; Eades, 1993, 1994; Shuy, 2006; Walsh, 1994), we can develop scientifically validated methods for authorship attribution and speaker identification (Bartle & Dellwo, 2015; Coulthard, 2000; Fraser, Stevenson, & Marks, 2012; Hammarström, 1987; Ishihara, 2017; Larner, 2014; Nini & Grant, 2013; Rose, 2013; Shaomin, 2016; Sørensen, 2012; Woolls & Coulthard, 1998), we can explain how to understand a trademark dispute or the semantic interpretation of a legal text (Aodha, 2017; Gibbons, 2012; Kaplan, Green, Cunningham, & Levi, 1995; Solan, 1998; van Naerssen, 2017). But progress has been achingly slow in achieving best practice and eliminating gross miscarriages of justice because again and again, justice and legal professionals are unwittingly making decisions that are outside their area of expertise (Ehrlich, Eades, & Ainsworth, 2016; Shuy, 2005).

This book is intended to contribute to an evidence-based approach to addressing language-related injustices in our legal system. It is presented as a series of case studies, but each chapter introduces readers to methods of data gathering and analysis that can be applied to research questions that arise in relation to the broad categories of forensic analysis for expert reports, police institutional discourse practices and general legal or regulatory language practices. While the findings of each of these projects or cases are themselves making a contribution to the field, the format of the chapters is designed to guide researchers through the process of researching forensic linguistic topics.

Why focus on researching forensic linguistics?

The forensic application of linguistics is most commonly realised through research. It is not a specialisation that can be acquired through undergraduate study alone. Students with comprehensive linguistics training take their first steps towards a career in forensic linguistics through a research thesis or dissertation focusing on language and the law. A PhD in linguistics is the minimum qualification for anyone providing expert forensic linguistics evidence in court, and similarly, a relevant research background is crucial for any academic pursuing a career in forensic linguistics at a university.

Yet many universities with strong linguistics departments do not seem interested in offering research supervision in forensic linguistics topics. Students who are unable to access one of the very few forensic linguistics centres or supervisors are naturally inclined to work in other areas of linguistics where they will be well supervised, with a range of topics available to them. As a result, despite decades of findings calling repeatedly for improvements to the way that language evidence and issues are treated in the justice system, the International Association of Forensic Linguists has seen remarkably slow growth in the field over the last 30 years. There is certainly no shortage of topics to be explored and problems to be addressed. Just within the narrow sub-specialisation of police cautions and consent-giving, Roger Shuy helpfully set out 'Ten unanswered language questions about Miranda' (Shuy, 1997) in order to encourage research into the American police cautioning of suspects. Despite several detailed and wide-ranging studies that have significantly contributed to our knowledge in this area (Ainsworth, 1993; Cotterill, 2000; Ehrlich et al., 2016; Heydon, 2016; see also Chapter 6 in this volume; Rock, 2007) most of these questions still remain unanswered 20 years later. Many other questions concerning language and the law have yet to be asked, or are being addressed in cognate disciplines, including psychology, criminology and police studies, without the benefit of systematic language analysis. Rather than competing with these disciplines, forensic linguists have the opportunity to collaborate and, together, produce a more comprehensive approach to the issues (see for instance Oxburgh, 2016). However, without an increase in the number of forensic linguists, we cannot adequately contribute a linguistic perspective in all the places it is needed.

Case studies and analysis

With this book, I hope to introduce academics and students to a range of approaches they can take to engage with the linguistic analysis of justice and legal problems. I have drawn on data sets collected over two decades of work in the field to offer ideas, inspiration and guidance in researching language across a variety of justice settings. For many readers, forensic linguistics is synonymous with giving expert evidence in a court trial. While this book will demonstrate that this is a narrow representation of the field, it provides a point of departure for our exploration of researching language and the law. As such, Part I presents case studies of forensic linguistic evidence used in criminal and civil proceedings. These two chapters focus on the expert reports presented in each trial; however, they both support the broader goal of this volume by showing how research remains the foundation of forensic case work. Several suggestions are made in both chapters for ways that further research might support and extend the capacity of experts to provide linguistic evidence.

Part II introduces three different research approaches to police institutional discourse, each of which emphasises the importance of collaboration with other academic disciplines and practitioners in the field. Such collaboration has greatly impacted my own research and as a result of my direct engagement with law enforcement agencies, my work on the language of police interviewing has evolved substantially from a purely linguistic treatise (Heydon, 2005b) to something more relevant to police practice (Heydon, 2012). Chapters 3 (Police Interviewing) and 4 (Lie Detection and Linguistics) demonstrate how a practitioner focus can be maintained without undermining a researcher's capacity to analyse the data critically. In Chapter 5 (Police Cautions and Comprehension), the critical examination of a police procedure is underpinned by the micro-level analysis of turn-taking. This more technical chapter is intended to show how discourse analytical tools can be applied in a police setting and might be useful to discourse analysts moving into forensic linguistics or supervising student researchers in the field.

Part III is intended to illustrate the variety of data sources and analytic approaches that are possible in forensic linguistic research. Chapter 6 suggests ways that linguistic analysis can support criminological research, which in my view is a relatively unexplored opportunity for cross-disciplinary collaboration. The chapter identifies a number of language-based research problems that emerged during a project investigating the online reporting of sexual assault (Heydon & Powell, 2018). Given the increasing international interest in research into the prevention of violence against women, it is important that linguists are involved in projects that use language data as the basis for analysis. Chapter 7 (Legal Investigative Interviewing) extends the application of practice-based knowledge from police interviewing to workplace investigations and presents a method of data gathering for the purpose of developing training materials, a common request from industry partners. Chapter 8 extends the reach of forensic linguistics still further by presenting an approach to field research aimed at developing resources for highly linguistically diverse societies to better manage communications in the justice system. The chapter also presents an example of collaboration between forensic linguists working on the same problems in vastly different parts of the world. Given the scarcity of forensic linguistic specialisation, such long-distance partnerships are vital to advance the field and increase the impact of our work. As this chapter proves, modern communications technology means that even researchers in remote corners of the globe like Melbourne can maintain a productive working relationship with a colleague in the heart of Africa.

A recurring theme in this volume is the availability of data for emerging researchers, or lack thereof. Several chapters present analyses of data sets that would likely prove inaccessible to students and even many established scholars struggle to access police interviews and court transcripts. Chapter 9 therefore presents a discussion of data collection methods that use publicly available data or laboratory-based data generation. Also included here is the outline of a project that introduces basic linguistic concepts of syntactic analysis through a fun mock-crime exercise for suitable school students. As I will discuss below, there are serious reasons for getting schools engaged in teaching scientific language analysis to young people, and forensic linguistics provides an ideal vehicle.

The paramount importance of ethical conduct in forensic linguistic research

Forensic linguistics case work inevitably raises some specific ethical considerations. Case work is typically undertaken by linguists as a private consultancy, rather than as an academic research project. Such work is therefore unlikely to be subject to the requirements of a university human ethics committee or institutional review board (IRB) (United States) but nonetheless should adhere to professional standards of practice.

The International Association of Forensic Linguists has developed a Code of Practice for expert linguistic witness and any FL expert report should adhere to those guidelines (IAFL, 2014). In addition, a case or a project that involves violent crimes or evidential material revealing intimate details of the parties raises other concerns. First among these is the need to balance respect for the people involved against one's own need for self-care. When analysing data and preparing a report, the expert must always keep in mind that they are dealing with the lives of real people. At all times, even in private, it is incumbent upon experts and analysts to treat the material and all the people it concerns with respect and dignity. Experts who are new to the field, and do not have a background in legal case work, might find themselves feeling strongly about the people involved in the case, or tempted to make jokes about the quality of the writing or the coherence of a speaker. But in a case like the Mackay murder (see Chapter 1), the dignity of the victim and her family, as well as the right of the suspect to be treated with respect, means that we must hold ourselves to a higher standard.

On the other hand, it is common in jobs that expose workers to potentially traumatising material or events that professionals develop distancing techniques to protect themselves from vicarious trauma. Self-care, as it is often termed in the social services fields, is an important aspect of our professionalism (Bessant, 2017). It is necessary to develop an approach to our forensic linguistic practice that avoids de-humanising the parties without becoming personally or emotionally involved in the circumstances of the case, at least to the extent that it causes us lasting harm.

It is natural to respond emotionally to the material we are asked to analyse, and our own humanity is enriched by our capacity for empathy. Recognising this, and acting to alleviate our own vicarious trauma, is therefore an important ethical consideration. Experts working on cases should ensure that they have access to counselling and resources for self-care programs. Where these are not available through the expert's workplace (e.g. their university), experts should identify suitable support services available to the public. Such services need to be confidential and accessible at times of need, and experts need to identify suitable support services *before* they take a case. Experts must never feel obligated to take a case that is likely to cause them harm. If, upon reviewing the material for a case, an expert finds that it is simply too difficult for them to work with, they must be able to decline the request for assistance. Senior experts who are leading teams of analysts would do well to keep this in mind and oversee the distribution of cases to avoid traumatic overload on any one analyst.

6 Introduction

Beyond the issues identified above relating to working on criminal cases, the key ethical concerns of the forensic linguist or researcher in a civil law case such as in Chapter 2 are the confidentiality of the client's case material. Perhaps it is even more important to emphasise this here, because the somewhat dry and impersonal nature of the case can lead an inexperienced analyst to be less concerned about the privacy of the parties involved. After all, there do not seem to be any deeply personal revelations or descriptions of violent or otherwise traumatising case details, and so document security might appear to be relatively unimportant. However, the fact remains that civil cases affect real people's lives, with the future of jobs or reputations often hanging in the balance. The inadvertent publication or disclosure of case facts could jeopardise a case just as surely as in a criminal case and the same effort must be made to safeguard the privacy of the parties concerned.

On the positive side, a great deal of information about corporations and business transactions is made publicly available in most countries, and this can be a useful source of contextual information either during the analysis (which would be rare for linguistic cases, but possible) or at a later stage for publication of the case analysis in a scholarly journal or book, as in this case.

Finally, even when the data for a research project can be found in the public domain, and there is not usually any requirement for ethics or IRB approval, there are still ethical considerations for the researcher. As with any research involving sensitive material, researchers need to take care that they are aware of the potential for vicarious trauma resulting from engaging with sexual assault literature and reporting websites, for example. As a professional working in the sector remarked during my own research in this field, 'you have to de-brief occasionally or you start thinking that the world's full of evil people.'

The impact of linguistic education in the broader community

To take an example well known to all sociolinguists, William Labov's work with the education department in New York was not only concerned with identifying that poor academic results in African-American students were resulting from they being taught in a variety of English that was unfamiliar to them (Labov, 1972). Labov's work was also instrumental in exposing the detrimental impact of teachers treating African-American English Vernacular as 'bad English.' In this high profile piece of research by one of the field's most well-known researchers, a technical differentiation between varieties of a language was clearly set out as an area that requires expert knowledge to identify and address. And yet, half a century has passed and still we have cases such as Gene Gibson's wrongful conviction for murder in Western Australia resulting from the police investigators believing that they were qualified to assess Gibson's English language proficiency. In Gibson's appeal, the judge found that

> [t]here is a significant possibility that answers given by the accused are unreliable because he did not understand what he was being asked, could not communicate his own thoughts adequately in English or gave false answers in order to appear agreeable.
>
> (The State of Western Australia v Gibson 2014)

Perhaps it seems a long way from the education of students in a New York school in the early 1960s to decisions about an Aboriginal man's language use in a remote police station in Australia in 2010, but between these two cases are a long list of forensic linguistic studies, findings, reports, recommendations and guidelines for legal professionals and police officers. In Australia alone, we have seen the Anunga rules (R v Anunga (1976) 11 ALR 412), specialised Aboriginal interpreter services (Allingham, 2006; Weis, 2001), Diana Eades' guidelines for questioning Aboriginal witnesses (Eades, 1992) and John Gibbons' work on revising the NSW police caution for interviews with suspects (Gibbons, 1994). In addition to these and other practical interventions, there have been hundreds of research projects conducted and articles published by linguists as well as specialists in cognate fields of interpreting and translating, law, criminology, sociology and police studies, many of which I have cited in this book. In countries around the world, similar lists can be made and there are countless examples of professional development courses delivered by linguists to translate all of this into practical advice. And yet, recent cases of language-related injustice like Gene Gibson's wrongful conviction demonstrate that this work is not reaching the right audience, or is being overlooked at the most crucial moment of decision-making.

Rather than restating the same problem in different words with different examples, I intended that this book might contribute to resolving this issue in a new way. It is clear that education is important but whereas most of the education efforts so far have been directed towards professional development for legal professionals, I believe we also need to raise awareness about language science in the broader public realm. Case studies in forensic linguistics described and cited in this volume suggest that many cases of wrongful conviction, questionable decision-making and unlawful procedures could be avoided if the application of language science in a legal context was part of general knowledge or if forensic linguistics had a similar status in the criminal justice system as forensic psychology, for instance. Psychology has long been a staple elective in schools and although psychologists might argue that pop psychology on daytime talk shows does more harm than good, at least people have heard of the discipline and might be inclined to consult an expert if something that appears to be a psychological problem occurs in the course of an investigation or court case. And when new cognitive or behavioural issues are identified, there is a recognised pathway for expanding the necessary education and procedures for justice professionals. Thus we now have family psychologists to assist in child custody cases, and intermediaries for people with cognitive impairment being interviewed by police. By comparison, Fraser (2018) has documented that it is extremely difficult to introduce an evidence-based reform of practice in the legal system that arises from a misunderstanding about how language works. We are starting from a position where legal practitioners don't know what they don't know. As Justice Peter Gray (ret.) has often pointed out, lawyers think that they *are* linguists (Gray, pers comm). Like many members of the public, lawyers and other legal and justice professionals often don't realise that there is a difference between the popular use of the term 'linguist' to mean someone who is clever with language or is multilingual, and the academic use of the term to mean the scientific approach to language analysis. As adept performers in rhetoric and argumentation, lawyers are indeed professional language users but this does not qualify them to give an expert opinion about language structure and use. This misconstrual of the very nature of linguistics by those outside the field leads to an almost intractable problem: not only are legal and justice institutions ill-equipped to provide linguistic expertise to address language-related problems, but they are also largely unaware that linguistic expertise even exists.

An education framework that sees linguistics as an essential tool for the teaching and learning of first languages would be a tremendously significant step towards justice for many people linguistically disadvantaged by the legal system. As mentioned in Chapter 9, linguistics is taught in some European universities as a part of the curriculum for English as a foreign language, but the real gap is in secondary education in Anglophone countries. There is some indication that this is changing, with a subject that includes some linguistic theory now being taught as an optional alternative to the standard English course in some senior high schools in Australia and Britain. In addition to the practical problem of finding teachers suitably qualified to teach a new curriculum, there is a strong cultural resistance to the teaching of linguistics by an education system that glorifies literature as the pinnacle of English studies. As a speaker at an English education conference recently, I noted that linguistics is regarded by many English teachers with disdain, as the formulaic or simplistic analysis of language that lacks both the creative heritage of literary criticism and the commercial appeal of media and communications studies.

To my mind, this is hardly a basis for a system of first language education and it has serious consequences. Students who are taught the basic concepts of linguistics, the core forms of analysis that are presently the topics of any first year linguistics unit, might at least recognise a linguistic barrier in the justice system when they see one. The police officers intending to interview Gene Gibson might have considered that his English language proficiency was not something that they were qualified to assess. Members in the Refugee Review Tribunal, upon repeatedly struggling to elicit relevant and detailed information from highly motivated but frustratingly confused applicants, might have seen that the problem was one of pragmatics, or at least language in some form. They might then have reached out to a linguist years ago, instead of engaging me almost by accident for some professional development training. Court interpreters might never have to deal with judges who insist on everything being 'just translated word for word' because they remember that each language is a complex system of meaning and equivalence between them is never perfect. And the Attorney-General's department would not be using SCAN to vet their security staff because they would know enough about how language works to know that changes in tense are unlikely to be a consistent marker of deception.

Adding linguistic topics to an already crowded curriculum is going to be a difficult task. But without an increase in the number of graduates and teachers with linguistic expertise, it is going to be impossible. I hope that this book will contribute to this project in three ways: first, to inspire more linguists and their research students to consider applying their analytic skills to legal and justice problems; second, to equip academics in cognate fields (law, criminology, social work and interpreting, for instance) to supervise or co-supervise students in forensic linguistic topics; and third, to encourage aspiring language teachers, especially first language teachers, to take up the challenge of forensic linguistic research as part of their studies, and incorporate linguistic analysis into their classrooms.

References

Ainsworth, J. (1993). In a different register: The pragmatics of powerlessness in police interrogation. *Yale Law Journal*, 103, 259–322.

Allingham, K. (2006). WA calls for statewide Aboriginal interpreter service. *Indigenous Law Bulletin*, 6(22), 6–7.

Aodha, M. M. (2017). New insights into the semantics of legal concepts and the legal dictionary. *International Journal of Speech, Language & the Law*, 24(2), 249–255. doi:10.1558/ijsll.34752

Auburn, T., Drake, S., & Willig, C. (1995). 'You punched him, didn't you?': Versions of violence in accusatory interviews. *Discourse and Society*, 6(3), 353–386.

Bartle, A., & Dellwo, V. (2015). Auditory speaker discrimination by forensic phoneticians and naive listeners in voiced and whispered speech. *International Journal of Speech, Language & the Law*, 22(2), 229–248. doi:10.1558/ijsll.v22i2.23101

Benneworth-Gray, K. (2014). 'Are you going to tell me the truth today?' Invoking obligations of honesty in police–suspect interviews. *International Journal of Speech, Language & the Law*, 21(2), 251–277. doi:10.1558/ijsll.v21i2.251

Bessant, J. (2017). Self-care in public and community sector workplaces. *International Journal of Public Administration*, 40(2), 126–137.

Conley, J. M., & O'Barr, W. M. (2005). *Just words: Law, language, and power* (2nd edition). Chicago: University of Chicago Press.

Cooke, M. (1996). A different story: Narrative versus 'question and answer' in Aboriginal evidence. *Forensic Linguistics: The International Journal of Speech, Language and the Law*, 3(2), 273–288.

Cotterill, J. (2000). Reading the rights: A cautionary tale of comprehension and comprehensibility. *Forensic Linguistics: The International Journal of Speech, Language and the Law*, 7(1), 4–25.

Coulthard, M. (2000). Whose text is it? On the linguistic investigation of authorship. In M. Coulthard & S. Sarangi (Eds.), *Discourse and social life* (pp. 270–287). London: Longman.

Coulthard, M., Johnson, A., & Wright, D. (2017). *An introduction to forensic linguistics: Language in evidence* (Second edition). Abingdon, Oxon: Routledge.

Eades, D. (1990). Language and the law: An Australian introduction. *Australian Journal of Linguistics*, 10, 89–100.

Eades, D. (1992). *Aboriginal English and the law: Communicating with Aboriginal English speaking clients: A handbook for legal practitioners*. Brisbane: Queensland Law Society.

Eades, D. (1994). A case of communicative clash: Aboriginal English and the legal system. In J. Gibbons (Ed.), *Language and the law* (pp. 234–264). Harlow: Longman Group.

Eades, P. P. (1993). The case for Condren: Aboriginal English, pragmatics and the law. *Journal of Pragmatics*, 20(2), 141–162.

Eastwood, J., & Snook, B. (2012). The effect of listenability factors on the comprehension of police cautions. *Law and Human Behavior*, 36(3), 177–183. doi:10.1037/h0093955

Ehrlich, S., Eades, D., & Ainsworth, J. (2016). *Discursive constructions of consent in the legal process*. Oxford, UK; New York, NY: Oxford University Press.

Eva Nga Shan, N. (2015). Judges' intervention in witness examination as a cause of omissions in interpretation in the Hong Kong courtroom. *International Journal of Speech, Language & the Law, 22*(2), 203–227. doi:10.1558/ijsll.v22i2.17782

Fraser, H. (2018). Covert recordings used as evidence in criminal trials: Concerns of Australian linguists. *Judicial Officers Bulletin, 30*(6), 53–56.

Fraser, H., Stevenson, B., & Marks, T. (2012). Interpretation of a crisis call: Persistence of a primed perception of a disputed utterance. *International Journal of Speech, Language & the Law, 19*(2), 261–292. doi:10.1558/ijsll.v18i2.261

Gibbons, J. (1990). Applied linguistics in court. *Applied Linguistics, 11*(3), 229–237.

Gibbons, J. (1994). *Language and the law*. Harlow: Longman Group.

Gibbons, J. (1996). Distortions of the police interview process revealed by video-tape. *Forensic Linguistics: The International Journal of Speech, Language and the Law, 3*(2), 289–298.

Gibbons, J. (2012). Towards a framework for communication evidence. *International Journal of Speech, Language & the Law, 19*(2), 233–260. doi:10.1558/ijsll.v18i2.233

Hale, S., Roque, M. S., Spencer, D., & Napier, J. (2017). Deaf citizens as jurors in Australian courts: Participating via professional interpreters. *International Journal of Speech, Language & the Law, 24*(2), 151–176. doi:10.1558/ijsll.32896

Hale, S. a., Napier, J., Hale, S. B. a., & Napier, J. (2013). *Research methods in interpreting a practical resource*. London, New York: Bloomsbury Academic.

Hammarström, G. (1987). Voice identification. *The Australian Journal of Forensic Sciences, 19*(3), 95–99.

Haworth, K. (2013). Audience design in the police interview: The interactional and judicial consequences of audience orientation. *Language in Society, 42*(1), 45–69. doi:10.1017/S0047404512000899

Heydon, G. (2002). The myth of the linguistic lie detector. *Monash University Linguistics Papers, 2*(2), 55–62.

Heydon, G. (2005a). Establishing the structure of police evidentiary interviews with suspects. *The International Journal of Speech, Language and the Law: Forensic Linguistics, 11*(1), 27–49.

Heydon, G. (2005b). *The language of police interviewing: A critical analysis*. New York: Palgrave Macmillan.

Heydon, G. (2005c). *The language of police interviewing – A critical analysis*. Houndmills, Basingstoke, Hampshire; New York: Palgrave Macmillan.

Heydon, G. (2012). Helping the police with their enquiries: Enhancing the investigative interview with linguistic research. *Police Journal: A Quarterly Review for the Police of the World, 85*(2), 101–122. doi:10.1350/pojo.2012.85.2.581

Heydon, G. (2013). From legislation to the courts: Providing safe passage for legal texts through the challenges of a police interview. In C. Heffer, F. Rock, & J. Conley (eds.), *Legal-lay communication: Textual travels in the law* (pp. 55–77). Oxford: Oxford University Press.

Heydon, G. (2016). Discursive constructions of consent in the legal process. *International Journal of Speech, Language & the Law, 23*(2), 301–306. doi:10.1558/ijsll.v23i2.32065

Heydon, G., & Powell, A. (2018). Written-response interview protocols: An innovative approach to confidential reporting and victim interviewing in sexual assault investigations. *Policing and Society, 28*(6), 631–646. doi:10.1080/10439463.2016.1187146

IAFL. (2014). International Association of Forensic Linguists Code of Practice. Retrieved from https://www.iafl.org/wp-content/uploads/2018/07/IAFL_Code_of_Practice_1-1.pdf

Ishihara, S. (2017). Strength of forensic text comparison evidence from stylometric features: A multivariate likelihood ratio-based analysis. *International Journal of Speech, Language & the Law, 24*(1), 67–98. doi:10.1558/ijsll.30305

Johnson, A. (2008). 'From where we're sat…': Negotiating narrative transformation through interaction in police interviews with suspects. *Text & Talk, 28*(3), 327–349. doi:10.1515/Text.2008.016

Johnson, A. J. (2008). Changing stories – Achieving a change of state in suspect and witness knowledge through evaluation in police interviews with suspects and witnesses. *Functions of Language, 15*(1), 84–114. doi:10.1075/fol.15.1.06joh

Jol, G., & van der Houwen, F. (2014). Police interviews with child witnesses: Pursuing a response with maar (= Dutch but)-prefaced questions. *International Journal of Speech, Language & the Law, 21*(1), 113–138. doi:10.1558/ijsll.v21i1.113

Kaplan, J. P., Green, G. M., Cunningham, C. D., & Levi, J. N. (1995). Bringing linguistics into judicial decision-making: Semantic analysis submitted to the Supreme Court. *Forensic Linguistics: The International Journal of Speech, Language and the Law, 2*(1), 81–98.

Labov, W. (1972). *Language in the inner city: Studies in the Black English vernacular.* Philadelphia: University of Pennsylvania Press, Incorporated.

Larner, S. (2014). A preliminary investigation into the use of fixed formulaic sequences as a marker of authorship. *International Journal of Speech, Language & the Law, 21*(1), 1–22. doi:10.1558/ijsll.v21i1.1

Licoppe, C., & Verdier, M. (2013). Interpreting, video communication and the sequential reshaping of institutional talk in the bilingual and distributed courtroom. *International Journal of Speech, Language & the Law, 20*(2), 247–275. doi:10.1558/ijsll.v20i2.247

Linell, P., & Jonsson, L. (1991). Suspect stories: On perspective setting in an asymmetrical situation. In I. Markova & K. Foppa (Eds.), *Asymmetries in dialogue* (pp. 75–100). Hemel Hempstead: Harvester Wheatsheaf.

Nakane, I. (2007). Problems in Communicating the Suspect's Rights in Interpreted Police Interviews. *Applied Linguistics, 28*(1), 87–112.

Nakane, I. (2011). The role of silence in interpreted police interviews. *Journal of Pragmatics, 43*(9), 2317–2330.

Napier, J., & Spencer, D. (2017). Jury instructions: Comparing hearing and deaf jurors' comprehension via direct or mediated communication. *International Journal of Speech, Language & the Law, 24*(1), 1–29. doi:10.1558/ijsll.30878

Nini, A., & Grant, T. (2013). Bridging the gap between stylistic and cognitive approaches to authorship analysis using Systemic Functional Linguistics and multidimensional analysis. *International Journal of Speech, Language & the Law, 20*(2), 173–202. doi:10.1558/ijsll.v20i2.173

Oxburgh, G. (2016). *Communication in investigative and legal contexts: Integrated approaches from forensic psychology, linguistics and law enforcement.* Chichester, West Sussex, UK: John Wiley & Sons.

Rock, F. (2007). *Communicating rights: The language of arrest and detention.* Houndmills: Palgrave Macmillan.

Rose, P. (2013). Where the science ends and the law begins: Likelihood ratio-based forensic voice comparison in a $150 million telephone fraud. *International Journal of Speech, Language & the Law, 20*(2), 277–324. doi:10.1558/ijsll.v20i2.277

Sapir, A. (1987). *The LSI course on scientific content analysis (SCAN).* Phoenix, AZ: Laboratory for Scientific Interrogation.

Shaomin, Z. (2016). Authorship attribution and feature testing for short Chinese emails. *International Journal of Speech, Language & the Law*, 23(1), 71–97. doi:10.1558/ijsll.v23i1.20300

Shuy, R. W. (1993). *Language crimes: The use and abuse of language evidence in the courtroom*. Cambridge, MA: Blackwell.

Shuy, R. W. (1996). *Language crimes: The use and abuse of language evidence in the courtroom*. Cambridge, MA: Blackwell Publishers.

Shuy, R. W. (1997). Ten unanswered questions about Miranda. *Forensic Linguistics: The International Journal of Speech, Language and the Law*, 4(2), 175–196.

Shuy, R. W. (2005). *Creating language crimes: How law enforcement uses (and misuses) language*. Oxford; New York: Oxford University Press.

Shuy, R. W. (2006). *Linguistics in the courtroom: A practical guide*. Oxford: Oxford University Press.

Smith, N. (2001). Reading between the lines: An evaluation of the Scientific Content Analysis technique (SCAN). *Police Research Series*, 135, 1–42.

Solan, L., M. (1998). Linguistic experts as semantic tour guides. *Forensic Linguistics: The International Journal of Speech, Language and the Law*, 5(2), 87–106.

Sørensen, M. H. (2012). Voice line-ups: Speakers' F0 values influence the reliability of voice recognitions. *International Journal of Speech, Language & the Law*, 19(2), 145–158. doi:10.1558/ijsll.v19i2.145

Svartvik, J. (1968). *The Evans statements: A case for forensic linguistics*. Göteborg: University of Goteborg.

van Naerssen, M. (2017). Translating the social world for law: Linguistic tools for a new legal realism. *International Journal of Speech, Language & the Law*, 24(1), 131–137. doi:10.1558/ijsll.33452

Vanderhallen, M., Vervaeke, G., & Mertens, E. (2008). *How do police officers with SCAN training perform in detecting lies?* Paper presented at the European Association of Psychology and Law Annual Conference, Maastricht.

Walsh, M. (1994). Interactional styles in the courtroom: An example from Northern Australia. In J. Gibbons (Ed.), *Language and the law* (pp. 217–233.). Harlow: Longman Group.

Weis, B. (2001). Northern territory Aboriginal interpreter service. *Indigenous Law Bulletin*, 5(8), 27.

Woolls, D., & Coulthard, M. (1998). Tools for the trade. *Forensic Linguistics: The International Journal of Speech, Language and the Law*, 5(1), 33–57.

Part I
Language crimes

1 Authorship attribution case file
Murder in Mackay

The case, like many others, began with a phone call from a detective.

'Hello? Dr Heydon? I'm a detective at Mackay CIB, Queensland Police. I am not sure if you're the right person, or if you can help me, but we've got a murder victim and an anonymous threatening letter and we think it was written by the suspect because the spelling is really similar...'

'Oh, right,' I think, 'spelling.' I sigh inwardly. 'OK, so you would like me to conduct an analysis to see if your suspect might be the same person who wrote the anonymous letter? Well, the thing about that is, spelling is almost never a very good indicator of authorship. It's just too similar across authors – even really bad spelling.'

But the detective was insistent: this was *really* unusual spelling, and it was consistent between the anonymous letter and all the written material he had gathered that was known to be written by the suspect. Could I just take a quick look?

The high profile case involved a young woman who died from serious injuries after being assaulted near her home. Her boyfriend was the prime suspect, despite having made a prominent appearance in a public march organised to honour the woman's memory and protest the violence and brutality of her death. Police were convinced the boyfriend had written the anonymous letter, which denounced the victim in graphic and explicit language as a poor lover and an unfaithful girlfriend. The prosecution case would rest in part on the attribution of the authorship of the letter to the suspect, on the basis that the letter was evidence of murderous intent. The suspect had denied writing the letter during his police interview.

I agreed to assess the evidence but I had already drafted the case rejection letter in my head before I'd put down the phone, and by the time the materials arrived on a disk sent by registered post, I had completely dismissed the request from my mind. And the reason I was so sure I couldn't help? As I had told the detective in Queensland, spelling is rarely a good indicator of authorship. But to understand why this is so, let's first understand more about this type of analysis.

Introduction

One of the most common types of forensic linguistic cases is the attribution of the authorship of a given text to an individual: authorship attribution. Typically, as in my Mackay case, the mystery text is an anonymous threatening letter, and it implicates the author in some kind of criminal activity or supports the case against them. In civil cases, a common need for authorship attribution arises in cases involving a contested will or other legal document. Forensic linguists in various jurisdictions have been involved in cases involving authorship attribution and it is a frequent topic of research published in the *International Journal of Speech, Language and the Law* and books on forensic linguistics (Coulthard, 2000; Gibbons, 2012; Larner, 2014; Nini & Grant, 2013; Perkins & Grant, 2018; Shaomin, 2016; Woolls & Coulthard, 1998) as well as computational linguistics and information technology. However, the origins of authorship attribution are neither legal nor linguistic. Historically, authorship attribution has been the realm of literary mysteries, perhaps most famously the authorship of the plays attributed to William Shakespeare (Trucco, 1988) and the Federalist papers (Mosteller & Wallace, 1963). In these literary cases, the methods used have evolved from largely stylistic analysis, where texts are described and compared with regard to various literary devices and historical context, to stylometric approaches such as word counts (Stamatatos, 2008). There is not the space here to provide a more complete overview of the many different approaches taken to authorship attribution; however, it is important to note that a considerable amount of work has been done in the computational linguistics and information science fields. Stamatatos (2008) provides a detailed description and critique of the various statistically or computationally supported methods of authorship attribution and the methods used to evaluate or test these methods.

Some approaches to forensic authorship attribution for legal matters use a non-statistical stylistic approach, and it is advocated in books by McMenamin, among others (McMenamin, 2002). However, several linguists have sharply criticized this method on the grounds that the features chosen for inclusion in the analysis are not selected for their known capacity to separate texts by different authors. For more on this, see David Crystal's critique of McMenamin (Crystal, 1995). Essentially, critics such as Crystal (1995) and Chaski (2001) find that stylistic analysis fails to address a central problem of authorship attribution: the problem of likelihood. For any feature that we might choose to analyse in the documents, we must be able to say how likely it is that the feature could not have been produced by some other author (Grant, 2007). Stylistic analysis does not attempt to calculate the statistical likelihood that the features identified in both known and questioned texts could have been produced by any other author.

This brings me back to the Mackay murder case, and the problem with spelling, or more properly, misspelling In ordinary, casual written documents, patterns of misspelling across different authors are so common that misspelling alone is almost always irrelevant as an identifying feature. Experience told me that the fact that the detective in Mackay had noticed the pattern of misspellings between the two sets of documents was not a strong indicator that they were written by the same person. I was very confident that, given a short amount of time and an internet connection, I could demonstrate that what might have seemed to be unusual patterns of misspelling were in fact extremely common. I would do this using a corpus-based method, as described below.

Approach to the problem

Authorship attribution relies on being able to correctly group together any texts produced by the same author. Therefore, the linguistic problem to be solved is to find features of the text that vary according to authorship. Sadly, however, there is no known 'text-fingerprint'[1] – a pattern of language use that is unique to each author. Stylistics describes patterns of language that are similar or different between two texts, but does not attempt to calculate how likely it is that these patterns of language might appear in any other author's texts. This means that a stylistic analysis has no statistical validity, which severely undermines its use in legal cases (Chaski, 2005). In the absence of a reliable and scientifically proven indicator of authorship, it is hard to see how such cases can be solved using linguistic analysis, although so many proposals are made for various computational methods that one is sure to emerge in the near future (Grieve, 2007; Stamatatos, 2008).

As should be clear to readers, I had no illusions about my capacity to provide a reliable finding in the Mackay case and I was especially sceptical of the detective's assurances that the spelling patterns in the documents would be the key. When non-linguists see spelling patterns as a strong indicator of authorship, they are generally unaware of what constitutes a common feature of language. For example, if both the known and questioned documents (QD) in a case included the word *cant* (*can't* without an apostrophe), this might appear to be a useful marker of authorship. In fact, a search of the Birmingham Blog (BB) Corpus, a collection of 630 million words drawn from blogging websites, shows that around 3.6% of instances of this word are spelled without the apostrophe, which makes it far from unusual.

When the data from the Mackay CIB arrived, I realised that I had misjudged the detective: these really were some of the most unusual spelling patterns I had ever seen, and it was clear right away that this would be one case where misspelling might be used to attribute authorship.

In the following sections I will describe how to undertake one form of corpus analysis for authorship attribution, how to present the findings for a lay audience and how this type of analysis can be applied to legal practice. Throughout this chapter, I will be using the Mackay case file to illustrate various aspects of this type of analysis. Before we turn to the method used to undertake the analysis of the data, we must first address the framing of the research question, and the collection of the data.

Identifying research questions

Like any research project, a forensic case needs a clear question to which the analysis and findings will provide a response. A forensic case is a very specific and focused kind of research project: the objective of the analysis is determined by a legal framework. In authorship attribution cases, the objective of the analysis is to test whether or not the documents in question were written by the same author. The primary research question therefore might be:

> Research Question 1. Does the linguistic analysis of the two data sets indicate that they were written by the same author?

In order to answer this question, we first need to answer at least two more questions:

> Research Question 2. What features of the data can be used to discriminate between the texts by the known author and texts by any other author?

and

> Research Question 3. What method can be used to analyse those features identified in Research Question 2 in order to produce valid results?

The terms of reference for the research questions need to be carefully defined, especially the scope of the term 'valid results.' For the purposes of providing an expert opinion, the validity of the research results will be determined in part by the court's rules relating to scientific evidence. There is a tendency for courts to prefer results that can be stated in a numerical form (Grant, 2007), which can be interpreted by the judge or jury as a percentage of probability that the proposition in question is true. In the Mackay case, the results would be described in terms of the likelihood that the two data sets were produced by the same person compared to the likelihood that the two data sets were produced by two different people. From this calculation, the court can determine the probability that the defendant authored the questioned letter, and not someone else. Note the difference between these two findings. The first can be determined using linguistic analysis and is the province of a linguistic expert. The second is determined using a common-sense analysis and is the province of the judge and/or jury (Coulthard, Johnson, & Wright, 2017; Gibbons, 2012; Grant, 2007).

Returning to the research questions that we have identified for this project, we might start with Question 2 ('What features of the data can be used to discriminate between the texts by the known author and texts by any other author?') and this brings us to the matter of data collection.

Data collection

In authorship attribution cases, the data available are usually supplied to the analyst by the police or lawyers. There might be times when it is possible or indeed necessary to specify the data required for the analysis, but mostly, the availability of data is predetermined by the facts of the case. This is especially true for the QD (see below). In relation to the documents of known or undisputed authorship, which I will refer to as KD (Known Document/s), there might be a large quantity of documents available, such as all the SMS texts from a mobile phone, or all the emails from an email account, or the quantity of material might be limited to only a handful of documents that were recovered from available sources and verifiably written by the suspect. In the case of the former, it is usual for the analyst to restrict the data set in some way, unless the method allows for a data set of limitless size. For example a computation analysis can be run on extensive data sets because the process is automated (Stamatatos, 2008). Whichever data selection criteria are applied, these need to be carefully documented and justifiable within the parameters of a valid analysis. In the Mackay case, there was no initial requirement to apply selection criteria to the data collection, as the police supplied all the available KD, although some complicating factors did arise in relation to one of the KD (see further below).

Typically, a case will involve a smaller set of texts – sometimes a single document – which are of unknown or disputed authorship. From here on I will refer to these texts as the QD. The availability of data in the QD set is usually limited but in some cases can be very extensive, such as where the case involves all the SMS texts from a mobile phone and the provenance or ownership of the phone itself is disputed. This is becoming more common in cases involving organised crime and terrorism where offenders use disposable mobile phones or SIM cards to avoid identification. In those cases, the data set required for the analysis might have to be defined and restricted using selection criteria, as described above for the KD data set.

In the Mackay case, the KD consisted of four texts produced by the suspect in response to a psychological self-help questionnaire (labelled KD1, KD2, KD3 and KD4), and approximately 850 text messages from the suspect's mobile phone (KD5). The authorship of these documents was not disputed by the defence. The QD for this case was an anonymous typed document approximately one and a quarter pages in length which was titled 'things about [name] i dont like' and consisted of a list of 28 statements about the victim and her relationship to the author. The language was highly explicit and the document referred mainly to sex acts and intimate details about the victim (see Ethical Considerations in Introduction).

Once the data sets are defined and obtained, the next task relevant to data collection is to identify the features for analysis whose similarities and differences across the two data sets will allow the findings to show how likely it is that the two data sets might have common authorship. This decision is closely related to the method being used for analysis, and it is therefore difficult to discuss one without pre-supposing the other. For instance, if the method to be used is computational or statistical analysis, then the material other than sentences (headings, greetings, emojis and so on) might need to be removed (Chaski, 2005; Stamatatos, 2008). For stylistic analysis, any feature of the text is potentially relevant but the selection task is in identifying features that stand out in some way as salient to the analyst. In some cases this might be any unusual features that appear in both QD and KD (McMenamin, 2002). Clearly this produces a biased sample, unless there is some statistical determination of the likelihood of these same features appearing in any random document.

The Mackay case involved a form of the latter: I identified instances of a salient characteristic common to the KD and the QD, and then I undertook further research to gather data on the likelihood of this characteristic appearing in any random document produced by a member of the general population (see Data Analysis below). As indicated earlier, the salient characteristic in the Mackay case documents was the use of misspelt words. More specifically, I identified words that used a form of spelling that I judged not to be non-standard nor typically non-target. That is, they were not deliberately misspelled (non-standard) like 'gonna' for 'going to,' *and* they were inadvertently misspelled (non-target) in a way that was not typical of misspellings in English. Of course, both of these judgements were based mainly on my experience and knowledge of the English language rather than evidence drawn from data analysis. We might also say that I used abductive reasoning to form an initial hypothesis. I observed that there were many instances of words in the QD that were spelled in a way I had not seen before, and which did not appear to be consistent with the features of Australian English or the common patterns of misspelling. For example, the word *can't* was produced several times as *carnt*. This struck me as unusual because misspelling is most often related to pronunciation: people misspell words because the written form of the word does not resemble the spoken form, or it is hard to determine the standard written form from the spoken form. Thus, it is common to misspell *accommodate* with one 'm' (**accomodate*) because it is impossible to determine from the sound of the word whether or not it has a double 'm.' But in the case of *can't* the sound of the word does not include the approximant 'r' so it is unlikely that a person would imagine that the spelling might be *carnt* on the basis of the sound of the word.[2]

I began the data selection by identifying all instances of apparently idiosyncratic non-target spellings in the QD. I then identified all instances of the target form, and any non-standard forms in the QD. I then carried out the same data selection on the KD; however, there were some complicating factors that reduced my selection to just four items that I used in the final analysis. The reason for this was explained in the report to the police:

> In the QD,[3] 74 instances of non-target forms were identified. Although most of these were also identified in KD5 (text messages), only four were selected for corpus analysis because a) they were also identified in the handwriting in KD1–4, and/or b) they were instances where a letter had been added to create the non-target form. These additional criteria addressed possibilities that the non-target production was a result of a keyboard error, or that the non-target form was an attempt to abbreviate the target form. The non-target forms were verified as present in the collection of text messages, however this document was not used in the final analysis. Although many tokens of the non-target forms were found in the document KD5, the readability of the document was so poor that some tokens were unidentifiable. Nonetheless, the verification of the non-target forms in KD5 was useful, given the size of that document, and indeed strongly supported the conclusion.

Data analysis

The data for the Mackay case could now be assembled ready for analysis. To manage the data, they were entered into a spreadsheet, which is reproduced here as Table 1.1, where I have included ten lines of original data for illustrative purposes.

Note that this table is not perfect: the third column was superfluous because in fact the list of non-target words in column 1 were all from the QD. Nonetheless, as a first cut of the data, this format allowed me to see which forms of the non-target words were present in both the QD and the KD. In this sample, we can see for instance that *cheeper/cheaper, *cheeted/cheated and *codeen/codeine did not appear in the KD at all, and that *cowincident only appeared as a variant form *qawincident in the KD. All such items were eliminated at this stage of the analysis.

The items that were relevant to the analysis, and would enable me to answer the research questions, were the ones that appeared in some form (non-target or target) in both data sets. Fortunately, the documents were reasonably consistent in register and genre (i.e. relating intimate personal problems), which improved the chances of the same words appearing across the two data sets (Chaski, 2005). In addition, many of the words listed in the first column were common words in English, and so this also increased the chances that they would appear in both the KD and the QD. Indeed, the fact that such common words were produced as non-target was one of the striking features of these texts.

As mentioned in data selection, above, I also eliminated non-target forms that might conceivably have been created inadvertently through mistyping the letters. For this reason, I eliminated *culdent, on the basis that it might have been formed by skipping the 'o' key.[4] I also eliminated forms that I could not identify in KD5, the set of text messages. Although almost all of the items were present in the KD5 data, I could not reliably identify them due to the poor quality of the typeface in that document. For example, the *carnt/karnt item, which was a prominent feature across all data sets, could not be reliably identified in KD5, because the

Table 1.1 Extract from the Mackay case data management spreadsheet showing ten lines of data (bold emphasis added)

Non-target word list	Target	Instances of non-target in QD	Instances of non-target in KD	Instances of target in QD	Instances of target in KD
ather	other	**ather**			
buy (as preposition)	by	**buy**			
carnt/karnt	cant/can't	carnt/karnt			
cheeper	cheaper				
cheeted	cheated				
codeen	codeine				
cowincident	coincidence	qawincident			
culdent/culdend	couldn't	culd/culdent			
gowing	going	**gowing**			
meany (adjective)	many	**meany**			

'r' letter was blurring into the 'n,' so that it was indistinguishable from an 'm' letter. This brings up one of the complicating factors that I mentioned earlier, and highlights the messiness of working with real-world data. KD5 was provided to me by the Mackay police as a tabulation of the text messages with their accompanying metadata. However, the document had been scanned from an original printout at low resolution and with very small fonts. The police had obtained the data from the mobile phone company in this poor quality format, and were unable to rectify the matter in this instance. I was therefore forced to be even more selective in my choice of items for analysis than I would have preferred. The remaining items are those highlighted with bold text in Table 1.1: *ather/other; *buy/by; *gowing/going, and; *meany/many. Note that *buy was not used in the verb form meaning to purchase, but as a non-target form of the preposition by.

Having identified these four items in the non-target word list suitable for further analysis, it then remained to identify how likely it was that the non-target forms in the QD might be produced by any random author, rather than the suspect. For this part of the analysis, it was necessary to compare the frequency of these items in the QD and KD, with their frequency in a large corpus of comparable text.

The selection of the corpus for this comparison needed to take into account the casual form of language used in the texts, and the interpersonal tone used in this genre of intimate letter or message writing and personal accounts. A corpus of newspaper articles, while readily available, would not yield examples of informal language and, most crucially, misspellings common to the case data. Instead, a more suitable corpus is the BB Corpus, a collection of 630 million words sourced from blogging websites and containing highly informal language and many non-target forms. As mentioned earlier, a search of the abbreviated form of can not finds that 3.6% of instances of can't in the BB Corpus are spelled without an apostrophe, which is indicative of the informal style of language found within it.

The first task of the analysis is to identify the frequency of each item in its non-target form, compared to its target form. Thus, I began by using the BB Corpus query form to search for each of the non-target forms. The BB Corpus query results are delivered in a concordance format, so that each instance of the item that is found in the corpus is presented with the four words that precede it and the four words that follow it in the source text. The results for the word *ather are presented in Figure 1.1.

Given the context of each instance of the non-target item, it is possible to see whether the search has yielded accurate results. For instance, the search of *ather yielded ten instances of this word; however, only one of them, item 5, was being used in context as a non-target form of other. The remaining nine instances were non-target forms of different words, several being instances of rather where the initial 'r' was either missing or separated by a space. There were 719,782 instances of the target form other in the BB Corpus.

The query form can also be used to narrow the search by grammatical function, which was necessary for the analysis of *buy. In order to differentiate the non-target use of *buy as the preposition by from the target form of buy as a verb, it was necessary to specify that I was searching for all instances of *buy as a preposition.

Authorship attribution case file 23

```
        10 instances of 'ather', case insensitive (0 min 1 sec).
 1:                             He opined that r ather than cooperation and dialogue,
 2:             Israeli conspiracy against Muslims. Ather Farouqui explains these types
 3:                             the night! Mother F - ather ! --------- Dave, these are
 4:                              real name either, r ather a nickname. Luckily we
 5:                           and zac what about ather black stars like keke
 6:                       fairness? Concludes Mock R ather than focusing on extending
 7:                           of President Obama R ather than caving in to
 8:                        and Gatorade or Powerade, ather than 'energy drinks' per
 9: Stores are hiring ... http://intensedebate.com/people/cthonctic Ather . I'm turned off of
10:                                a teamate i would ather have a hussle player

                               Showing results 1 to 10
```

Figure 1.1 Screenshot from the Birmingham Blog Corpus showing concordance results for *ather*.

Table 1.2 Final results of the data analysis for Mackay authorship attribution case

Forms	Instances in QD	Instances in KD1–4	Corpus	Identified in KD5
*ather ADJ	1	1	1	Yes
other	0	0	719,782	
*gowing VB	1	1	7	Yes
going	0	0	680,552	
*meany ADJ	2	1	0	Yes
many	0	0	484,263	
*buy PREP	2	2	0	Yes*
by	0	0	2,197,260	

* The item was tentatively identified in KD5 but the poor quality of the text made it difficult to identify the letter characters with absolute certainty.

Alternatively, one could use refined search terms and identify all instances of *buy* as NOT VERB. The search of the BB Corpus yielded no instances of *buy* as a preposition, but 2,197,260 instances of the target form *by* as a preposition.

Similarly, the non-target item **meany* as an adjective (target: *many*) needed to be differentiated from possible spellings of the juvenile term *meanie* as a noun (i.e. someone who is mean). Using these parameters with the BB Corpus yielded no instances of the non-target form **meany* but 484,263 instances of the target *many*.

Finally, there were seven instances of the non-target form **gowing* found in the BB Corpus. Interestingly, in several cases these were texts that were intended to represent the sound of a regional variety of British English.

There were 680,552 instances of *going* in the BB Corpus however, so the frequency of the non-target form was still not high.

The final results of the data analysis are summarised in Table 1.2.

Interpreting the findings

In this case, the findings show that the non-target forms appeared consistently in the QD and the KD, but very infrequently or not at all in the corpus of informal language from Blog websites. For each of the four items analysed previously, they only appeared in their non-target form in the (legible) case material and there were no instances of the items appearing in their target form. This is important, because we need to be concerned not just with the appearance of an unusual item, but the chances of it appearing in place of the standard or target form. Thus, we can say that in every place where the item was used, it was used by the author/s of the KD and the QD in its non-target form.

When we compare this to the corpus data, the differences are stark. For two of the items, the non-target form is never used by any author in any of the hundreds of thousands of instances of the item being used. No author of any of the 630 million words in the BB Corpus has ever used the form *meany* when they intended to write *many*, or produced the preposition *by* with a 'u': *buy*. On only one occasion has an author in the BB Corpus produced *other* as *ather*, and on only seven occasions out of nearly one hundred thousand times that number has an author produced the word *going* with an inserted 'w': *gowing*, and then mostly to create a specific literary effect, which is arguably not non-target at all.

These findings suggest that the non-target forms contained in the QD and the KD are so unusual that it would be difficult to find another author who might have written them amongst the many hundreds of thousands of authors that have contributed to the 630 million-word BB Corpus. Exactly how difficult though? One way of expressing the findings is that there is a 100% chance of the author using the non-target forms of each of these items in the KD and the QD, compared to a miniscule chance (0.0000014% for *ather* and 0.00001% for *gowing*; 0% for *meany* and *buy*) of any author using these forms in the BB Corpus. On this basis, we might conclude that the chance is close to zero that the KD was produced by the suspect and the QD was produced by one of the random samples represented by the hundreds of thousands of people contributing to the BB Corpus. Note that we can never rule out the possibility of separate authors completely. The BB Corpus is very large but there still remains a remote possibility that another author exists with the same idiosyncratic writing characteristics. Moreover, the sample sizes of the KD and the QD are small, and it is possible that given longer texts, the author/s might produce target forms of the items we analysed. On the other hand, most of the texts that form the BB Corpus are not long either, and an extremely large sample of authors is represented by the 630 million words. Additionally, the words we analysed are common, and appeared many hundreds of thousands of times in the BB Corpus, so we did not want for potential non-target forms; they simply did not appear with anything like the frequency that the QD and the KD would predict.

In this case, I did not go any further with my findings than the conclusions I have presented here. I left the final decision with the judge and jury as to whether they found the numbers compelling, alongside all the explanation of the analysis and the data used in it.

In the trial, the defence counsel admitted that the defendant had indeed written the anonymous letter that denigrated and humiliated the victim in the most aggressive and inhumane manner before she died from a violent assault a few blocks from her home. However, the decision not to contest the authorship of the anonymous letter (it had been contested at the pretrial hearing) meant that my expert testimony was never required. Thus it is impossible to know what the court might have concluded from the analysis, but the report might have had an influence on the decision of the defence counsel to admit to the letter's authorship. The defendant was eventually found not guilty of murder, but his authorship of the anonymous letter was confirmed.

Applications to legal practice and procedures

Most obviously, authorship attribution can provide evidence in criminal or civil cases where, like the Mackay case, there is a document of contested authorship, and this document contributes to the legal argument being made in the case. In the Mackay case, the prosecution case rested in part on linking the writing of the abusive letter to the victim and her subsequent murder. The defence case regarding the letter was simply that writing an abusive letter did not prove the defendant had committed murder. Note that this case did not involve any kind of profiling of the author or threat assessment: the police were not requesting that I answer the question of whether or not the author of the letter might have murdered the addressee.

The legal application of authorship attribution might be straightforward and obvious but the practice of authorship attribution is much more controversial than this case suggests. As stated in the introduction to this chapter, there is not yet any reliable and widely applicable method of authorship attribution. Methods that rely on the analyst's own experience or beliefs about language use and are not supported by any kind of systematic analysis of comparable data sets are of little use to courtrooms or police investigations.[5] The method described in this chapter can only rarely be applied, for all the reasons stated earlier. There have been some advances using computational methods, of which corpus analysis represents one of the simpler types, and I refer interested researchers to the recent work on computational and statistical methods (Stamatatos, 2008) as these approaches seem most likely to provide statistically reliable and valid results. However, there is a growing need for reliable authorship analysis, as the world has become more, not less, dependent on text-based communications. This is the case, not only in criminal courtrooms but also in civil matters such as unmasking the authors of hurtful and abusive anonymous posts on social media platforms. Governments and security agencies too have a powerful need for a reliable method of attributing authorship.

This gap in our capacity to provide expertise is perhaps one of the most obvious topics for research in forensic linguistics. Indeed, it is somewhat puzzling that this clearly identifiable problem has not yet been resolved, since the benefits are so obvious. Perhaps it is such an obvious research topic that potential researchers assume it has already been satisfactorily addressed!

26 *Language crimes*

This chapter has suggested several possible approaches to a research project that addresses the problem of authorship attribution. The method must be replicable and applicable to typical case data. Others have written extensively about these criteria (Chaski, 2001; Grant, 2007; Kredens & Coulthard, 2012), but the key point they make is that any method that is to work must be applicable to a wide range of text types and must be tested using validated ground-truth data sets. Forensic authorship attribution can involve large collections of micro-texts (SMS texts, Tweets, Facebook posts and so on), but can also involve large quantities of mid-length texts (email messages, letters and sworn documents). On the other hand, the QD is sometimes very short. The texts can include non-alphanumerical characters, which can be used with grammatical and semantic meaning, and the texts might accompany, and refer to, images. The use of mobile platforms can influence the text production process, as can auto-correct functions.

Many of these aspects of electronic text-based communications are covered in recent research papers (Grieve, 2007; Ishihara, 2017; Johnson, 1997; Kredens & Coulthard, 2012; Marko, 2017; Nini, 2017; Perkins & Grant, 2018; Shaomin, 2016; Shunichi, 2014; Wright, 2013) but as yet, there has not been a unifying theory or method for authorship attribution that accounts for all these elements systematically. For the dedicated researcher or student seeking a potentially groundbreaking project, authorship attribution offers exceptional opportunities for applied linguistic research. The same three research questions, as addressed in this chapter, can be used to guide such a project:

> Research Question 1. Does the linguistic analysis of the two data sets indicate that they were written by the same author?
> Research Question 2. What features of the data can be used to discriminate between the texts by the known author and texts by any other author?
> Research Question 3. What method can be used to analyse those features identified in Research Question 2 in order to produce valid results?

Final word

One aspect of this case that puzzled me was how anyone could produce such idiosyncratic spelling, and yet still write complex and coherent sentences. Additionally, there were examples of words that are commonly misspelt but which this author had correctly produced. This text production didn't seem to be consistent with anything I knew about language acquisition and use, and the analysis itself demonstrated the distinctiveness of the writing. When I had concluded my report and submitted it to the Mackay detective, I asked about the circumstances of the case. The detective told me that the defendant was a professional boxer, and that at the time of the murder, he had been seeking counselling for his erratic moods. He was apparently concerned that he was experiencing cognitive degeneration, most probably related to boxing injuries. This suggested that a logical explanation for these highly idiosyncratic patterns of language use was that they were produced by someone with an acquired brain injury, which is known to affect language production (Ylvisaker, Turkstra, & Coelho, 2005). While not relevant to my analysis, it was satisfying to tie up this 'loose end.'

Notes

1 Chaski (2013) claims that a combination of markedness, syntactically classified punctuation and sentence length can be used to accurately sort texts according to authorship; however, the algorithm used to calculate the results of the analysis is subject to a patent application in the United States.
2 There is one rational explanation though: words like *cart* that have a post-vocalic 'r' in some varieties of English, most commonly General American English, are not pronounced with the 'r' in Australian English. The Australian English writer cannot rely on the sound of the word to find the spelling, and must simply remember that the word has a silent 'r.' However, while the 'r' is not present as an approximant, its inclusion in the spelling does influence the vowel, such that it becomes an open front unrounded vowel rather than a mid front unrounded vowel (as in *cat*). There is therefore a kind of logic to the 'r' insertion in *carnt* as a way of 'explaining' the lowering (lengthening) of the vowel that occurs between *can* and *can't* in Australian English. Nonetheless, it is not a phenomenon that I have ever observed before.
3 In the original report, I had used a different coding scheme for the documents but for the sake of consistency in this text, I have converted the coding to the QD/KD format.
4 It is true that the non-target '-ent' suffix would have fitted my criteria, as it contains an inserted 'e' and appears in KD and QD, but for the purposes of writing an expert report for a non-specialist audience, I chose to use only whole words in the analysis.
5 Although as indicated earlier in this chapter and noted by Crystal (1995) and others (Chaski, 2001), there are still practitioners of such descriptive and non-statistical methods providing expert reports in cases despite no evidence of linguistic method or training.

References

Chaski, C. E. (2001). Empirical evaluations of language-based author identification techniques. *Forensic Linguistics*, 8, 1–65.
Chaski, C. E. (2005). Who's at the keyboard? Authorship attribution in digital evidence investigations. *International Journal of Digital Evidence*, 4(1), 1–13.
Chaski, C. E. (2013). Best practices and admissibility of forensic author identification. *Journal of Law and Policy*, XXI(2), 333–376.
Coulthard, M. (2000). Whose text is it? On the linguistic investigation of authorship. In M. Coulthard & S. Sarangi (Eds.), *Discourse and social life* (pp. 270–287). London: Longman.
Coulthard, M., Johnson, A., & Wright, D. (2017). *An introduction to forensic linguistics: Language in evidence* (second edition). Abingdon, Oxon: Routledge.
Crystal, D. (1995). Book review. [Forensic Stylistics, Gerald R. McMenamin]. *Language*, 71(2), 381–385. doi:10.2307/416174
Gibbons, J. (2012). Towards a framework for communication evidence. *International Journal of Speech, Language & the Law*, 19(2), 233–260. doi:10.1558/ijsll.v18i2.233
Grant, T. (2007). Quantifying evidence in forensic authorship analysis. *International Journal of Speech, Language & the Law*, 14(1), 1–25. doi:10.1558/ijsll.v14i1.1
Grieve, J. (2007). Quantitative authorship attribution: An evaluation of techniques. *Literary and Linguistic Computing*, 22(3), 251–270.

Ishihara, S. (2017). Strength of forensic text comparison evidence from stylometric features: A multivariate likelihood ratio-based analysis. *International Journal of Speech, Language & the Law*, 24(1), 67–98. doi:10.1558/ijsll.30305

Johnson, A. (1997). Textual kidnapping-a case of plagiarism among three student texts? *The International Journal of Speech, Language and the Law*, 4(2), 210–225.

Kredens, K., & Coulthard, M. (2012). Corpus linguistics in authorship identification. In L. M. Solan & P. M. Tiersma (Eds.), *The Oxford handbook of language and the law* (pp. 504–516). Oxford, UK: Oxford University Press.

Larner, S. (2014). A preliminary investigation into the use of fixed formulaic sequences as a marker of authorship. *International Journal of Speech, Language & the Law*, 21(1), 1–22. doi:10.1558/ijsll.v21i1.1

Marko, K. (2017). Strategies for disguise in written threatening communications and ransom demands: An analysis of English and German texts. *International Journal of Speech, Language & the Law*, 24(2), 243–247. doi:10.1558/ijsll.35084

McMenamin, G. R. (2002). *Forensic linguistics: Advances in forensic stylistics*. Boca Raton, FL: CRC Press.

Mosteller, F., & Wallace, D. L. (1963). Inference in an authorship problem. *Journal of the American Statistical Association*, 58(302), 275–309. doi:10.1080/01621459.1963.10500849

Nini, A. (2017). Register variation in malicious forensic texts. *International Journal of Speech, Language & the Law*, 24(1), 99–126. doi:10.1558/ijsll.30173

Nini, A., & Grant, T. (2013). Bridging the gap between stylistic and cognitive approaches to authorship analysis using systemic functional linguistics and multidimensional analysis. *International Journal of Speech, Language & the Law*, 20(2), 173–202. doi:10.1558/ijsll.v20i2.173

Perkins, R., & Grant, T. (2018). Native language influence detection for forensic authorship analysis: Identifying L1 Persian bloggers. *The International Journal of Speech, Language and the Law*, 25, 1–20.

Shaomin, Z. (2016). Authorship attribution and feature testing for short Chinese emails. *International Journal of Speech, Language & the Law*, 23(1), 71–97. doi:10.1558/ijsll.v23i1.20300

Shunichi, I. (2014). A likelihood ratio-based evaluation of strength of authorship attribution evidence in SMS messages using N-grams. *International Journal of Speech, Language & the Law*, 21(1), 23–49. doi:10.1558/ijsll.v21i1.23

Stamatatos, E. (2008). A survey of modern authorship attribution methods. *Journal of the Association for Information Science and Technology*, 60(3), 538–556.

Trucco, T. (1988). Bard on trial again, and again he wins. (Mock trial disputes authorship of Shakespeare's plays). *New York Times*, 138, B1.

Woolls, D., & Coulthard, M. (1998). Tools for the trade. *Forensic Linguistics: The International Journal of Speech, Language and the Law*, 5(1), 33–57.

Wright, D. (2013). Stylistic variation within genre conventions in the Enron email corpus: Developing a textsensitive methodology for authorship research. *International Journal of Speech, Language & the Law*, 20(1), 45–75. doi:10.1558/ijsll.v20i1.45

Ylvisaker, M., Turkstra, L. S., & Coelho, C. (2005). *Behavioral and social interventions for individuals with traumatic brain injury: A summary of the research with clinical implications*. Paper presented at the Seminars in speech and language.

2 Legal language interpretation case file
Solvency and semantics

> Like most professionals in the legal world, sometimes I am asked to take on cases that are distasteful, disturbing or just downright unappealing. As a forensic linguist, I have the luxury of choice, and I have already mentioned that I would avoid a case that is likely to cause unmanageable vicarious trauma. When I was first approached by a lawyer seeking my expert opinion in a bankruptcy case, I faced a similar dilemma. However, the only risk I faced was terminal boredom. Perhaps the legal nuance of bankruptcy and solvency is exciting to some; my father was apparently passionate about corporate law, so I admit the possibility. But nothing puts me to sleep faster than the phrase 'protracted legal battle involving irregularities in the book-keeping.' Sadly, this risk did not seem adequately threatening to my well-being to preclude me from taking the case, and so began my first foray into the forensic linguistics of civil law. The case I present here involved the interpretation of a specific phrase in a Court Order and it is intended to illustrate some of the pitfalls and frustrations faced by linguists who seek to provide expert opinions about the language of legal documents. Happily for the linguist, the tedium of the legal context can be largely ignored during the analytic phase, and indeed, legal phraseology can provide a fascinating array of semantic and syntactic puzzles. The real challenge lies in persuading the court that this linguistic evidence constitutes *expertise*, and is not *common knowledge* about language. This tends to come as a nasty shock to those of us who have spent hours grappling with x-bar theory, or wading through Chomsky's treatise on universal grammar, but to non-linguists, especially legal professionals, it is apparently unproblematic to assume that they have complete knowledge of how language works.

Introduction

In consideration of the interpretation of legal texts we need to make a clear distinction between the legal interpretation of a document and a linguistic interpretation of the language in the document. However, almost immediately, it is apparent that this is a much more difficult task than might be imagined. Indeed, in the case study I present here, the judge hearing the evidence was unable to make this distinction at all, and considered that my linguistic definition of the problem fell within his purview as deciding legal questions.

In civil law, many cases are based on arguments about the interpretation of contracts or other legally binding texts. Sometimes, this concerns the authorship of the text, and this is more straightforwardly a problem for a forensic linguist applying a method such as that described in Chapter 2. However, a great deal of court time in civil cases is devoted to arguments over the meaning of the words or phrases in a specific segment of a document (Aodha, 2017; Kaplan, 2016). In international trade negotiations, this has led to the creation of powerful tribunals whose members decide on the appropriate translation of multilingual trading contracts between nations or corporations. Increasingly, such tribunals are calling on linguistic expertise (Bhatia, 1983; Merkel et al., 2016). Thus, alongside the corporate world of trade and contract law experts there is a growing academic field of *legal semiotics* that combines semantics, syntax, discourse analysis and translation theory with legal expertise to produce guidelines and advice for government and corporate negotiators (Bhatia, Candlin, & Engberg, 2008). While there is some overlap between the legal semiotics community and the forensic linguistics community, the two fields are regarded as distinct, with legal semiotics being more clearly a branch of legal study, while forensic linguistics is regarded as an application of linguistic theory to a specific (legal) area of professional practice (Grewendorf & Rathert, 2009). The case I present here, which analyses the meaning of a phrase in a bankruptcy court decision, is at its core a linguistic problem that does not address broader legal concerns about the language of this type of document. It is therefore less a part of legal study, and more a language problem that happens to arise in a legal case. Nonetheless, as mentioned above, it was not possible to convince the judge that a linguist might be able to offer a useful interpretation of the data.

Approach to the problem

In this case, the lawyer had approached me about a Federal Court case involving bankruptcy and, more specifically, a complex set of circumstances surrounding his client's access to various bank accounts. The lawyer seemed to have reached a point of desperation as the case had become more and more drawn out, and his client was now accused of disobeying an Order made by a judge in an earlier hearing, specifically, that he had accessed money in certain bank accounts contrary to a Court Order. While there was no dispute about the defendant's actions – he had indeed withdrawn money from the bank accounts – the defence was seeking to show that the wording of the Order was sufficiently ambiguous that the defendant believed he was not acting unlawfully. Specifically, the defence claimed that the Order only referred to money that was in the bank accounts at the time the Order was made, and not to money that was deposited in the accounts at a later date. Thus, the defendant was, according to the defence's interpretation of the Order, free to withdraw money from the accounts, as long as the balance did not fall below the amount that was in the accounts when the Court Order was made. Whether or not this was the intent of the judge making the Orders (clearly, it was not!), the defence lawyer who contacted me was seeking my expert opinion about the linguistic viability of such an interpretation of the legal text. Thus, the forensic linguistic analysis focused only on a specific phrase used in the Order where it described the relevant funds as 'moneys standing to the credit of [bank accounts held by the defendant and his associates].'

Identifying research questions

While there are a number of questions that might arise concerning the comparative reasonableness of various interpretations, my task in this case was merely to describe one particular interpretation of the text and whether or not it was linguistically viable. The forensic analysis needed to consider whether or not the phrase used in the Order – 'moneys standing to the credit of [bank accounts held by the defendant and his associates]' – would be reasonably interpreted to mean that the word 'moneys' referred only to funds in the relevant accounts at the time that the Order was made, and not to any future funds credited to the accounts. In other words, one of the research questions for this investigation was:

> What is the time period denoted by the phrase?

Secondary, supporting questions that arise are:

> What are the syntactic units of the phrase relevant to determining the denotation of a time period?
> Do these syntactic units denote only a completed time period in the past, or an ongoing time period extending indefinitely into the future?

As mentioned, this case study did not include an analysis of the reasonableness of one interpretation over another, but if it had, then the research questions would need to reflect this. A research question that might be formed is:

> How much more common is one interpretation than another?

Data collection

The data for legal language interpretation cases are invariably supplied by the legal team. In this case, the lawyer supplied the entire Order, but drew my attention to the relevant paragraph. It is particularly important that the data are supplied with their original formatting and surrounding context intact. Legal texts are commonly set out in numbered paragraphs or sections, with many items governed syntactically by a verb phrase in a header text. Sometimes, such itemised lists are not set out in a list format, but appear as a paragraph, as in this example from Victoria, Australia in a draft version of the Family Violence Intervention Order coversheet:

> Important: Children can experience long-term harm if they see, hear or are exposed to family violence. This includes knowing that it is happening even if they are not there at the time. It includes seeing damaged property or injured people; knowing one parent is afraid of or controlled by the other; knowing that the family is controlled by one parent's behaviour and moods; and intervening to protect a parent or calm one down. It also includes unborn babies experiencing their mother's fear and stress during pregnancy.

As this example demonstrates, it is important that any governing propositions are included in the data set for analysis, even when the connection to the relevant text is not obvious. Here, there is a complex grammatical structure where the governing proposition in the first sentence is used to set up the category relevant to the subsequent list of items. That category is something like 'things that can cause long-term harm to children exposed to family violence.' The deictic anaphoric marker 'this' at the start of the second sentence and the anaphoric 'it' at the start of the third sentence refer the reader to the first sentence, specifically to the subordinated clause in sentence-final position. It is unclear what the anaphoric '[i]t' at the start of the fourth sentence refers to. Hypothetically, if a defendant in a family violence case exposed his/her children to one of the items listed in this paragraph, and then claimed that they did not understand that this was a proscribed action, a forensic linguist might be tasked with demonstrating that the grammatical relationships between the clauses were consistent with the intent of the law. In this particular case, I imagine that this might be quite difficult because the grammatical relationships are very complex and require considerable pragmatic assumptions on the part of the reader. In fact, my advice to the relevant Court was that this text be revised before publication to remove these ambiguities, and an alternative version was provided. This demonstrates the importance of involving a forensic linguist in the early stages of drafting Orders or legislation.

Returning to the case study in this chapter, the contextual data supplied in the full copy of the Order indicated that the object of the phrase 'moneys standing to the credit of…' was 'bank accounts held by the defendant and his associates.' Moreover, the complete set of documents did not provide any further indication about the intention of the Order to refer to a bounded time period or an indefinite, ongoing time period. Thus, the research questions set out previously were suitable for the analysis in light of all available and relevant data.

Data analysis

As indicated by the research questions above, the overriding objective of this analysis is to establish the time period denoted by the phrase 'moneys standing to the credit of...' The two sub-questions provide guidance for the direction of the analysis and so the initial task in this analysis is to identify

> What are the syntactic units of the phrase relevant to determining the denotation of a time period?

Semantic information about *time* is encoded in verbs through their aspect and this information can be modified or augmented using an adverbial phrase that specifies the actual time of the event referred to by the proposition. In the sentence 'I went to the shop yesterday' the verb TO BE is presented in the past perfect aspect WENT, indicating that the action being described is completed and occurred in the past. The adverbial phrase 'yesterday' indicates that the action was completed the day prior to the time of the utterance. Verb aspect is complex in English, but in standard written English, it is generally unambiguous. Exceptions in non-standard English might be the use of 'present historical,' where a present tense form is used to denote a past time, often in a narrative: 'So I'm walking down the street and this guy comes up to me and pushes me into the gutter.' The action being described can logically only have occurred in the past relative to the time that the story is being told, but the verbs are all constructed using the present continuous or simple present forms. However, in a legal document written in standard English, we would not expect to find this use of the present historical, and so we can ascertain the time period denoted by phrase by identifying the aspect of the main verb. In this case, the relevant verb – 'standing' – is expressed as part of an adjectival phrase that describes the noun 'moneys' in 'moneys standing to the credit of...'

This brings us to the second sub-question:

> Do these syntactic units denote only a completed time period in the past, or an ongoing time period extending indefinitely into the future?

As mentioned, the semantic interpretation of the adjectival phrase 'standing to the credit of' rests in the aspect of the verb form 'standing.' In order to analyse this phrase, we first need to expand the phrase from its current form, which contains an ellipsis, or reduction of the grammatical elements. A simple example of ellipses is the contraction in 'don't' where the two words in the full form 'do not' are contracted to an elliptical form that reduces the second syllable and joins the two words into a single unit. In the phrase 'the moneys standing to the credit of...' there is an underlying, implied form that has the structure 'the moneys that are standing to the credit of...' By expanding the phrase, we can more readily identify the form of the verb 'standing' in the adjectival phrase as:

TO BE + stand + ING.

This form of the verb is the present progressive. By reference to an authoritative text on English semantics, preferably something accessible to a lay audience, we can provide a clear description of what this grammatical form means. In the case report I prepared for this analysis, I referred the Court to a high quality but accessible textbook 'Introducing English Semantics' by Charles W. Kreidler (Kreidler, 1998). The present progressive is described by Kreidler (1998) as a temporary or bounded form. Kreidler further notes that: 'the present progressive is used for what is temporarily true.' Thus, the activity 'standing to the credit of' is confined to a bounded period of time – it does not extend indefinitely. For the purposes of clarity, I included in my report a comparison between this use of the present progressive and the simple present. I explained if the phrase included the simple present aspect of the verb 'stands to the credit of,' this would express a durative activity, something that may continue to be true.

In conclusion, the semantic analysis of the questioned text finds that the phrase 'the moneys standing to the credit of' could be reasonably interpreted by the addressee to mean that the moneys are those standing to the credit of the relevant accounts at the time that the words were written – that is, the date of the Order or, at the latest, the date of the Order being read by the addressee.

To return to the point made previously about the reasonableness of the interpretation, this too might be addressed through linguistic analysis. I will not present such an analysis here, as it did not form part of this case file; however, it is worthwhile taking the time to consider how such an analysis might be accomplished, since it becomes relevant to the interpretation of the findings below. For a linguist, there are two main methods we might use to establish how 'reasonable' a particular meaning or interpretation might be, both of which relate 'reasonableness' to usage. First, we might seek historical information about how such a phrase has been used or understood in the past. While the phrase 'standing to the credit of' is unlikely to arise in ordinary conversation, it might occur regularly in banking texts, or legal documents, such as the Order in this case. Therefore, there might be some value in conducting a survey of such texts by collecting a corpus of samples and identifying through the contextual detail, how the phrase has been applied in similar linguistic environments in the past. The second approach that might be used to establish 'reasonableness' is a survey of usage by participants who complete a questionnaire or discourse completion task (Billmyer & Varghese, 2000; Félix-Brasdefer, 2010). By collecting data about how the phrase has been interpreted in the past or how a sample set of participants are most likely to interpret the phrase in a questionnaire, we could provide quantitative findings that describe how reasonable it is to interpret the phrase in a particular way.

Interpreting the findings

This case study presents a fairly straightforward linguistic analysis, referring only to elementary semantic theory and not involving complex computation or comparison. As indicated, a further layer of complexity might be added by a survey of usage to provide a response to the question of 'reasonableness' and this might go some way towards addressing the issues raised below about the distinction between the legal and the linguistic opinions on the interpretation of legal texts. However, as the discussion below explains, there is a further level of analysis that might yet be added to the case, which is the question of 'intent' versus interpretation. In fact, this entire case can be usefully considered in relation to concentric circles of analyses, as in Figure 2.1.

At the outer level in Figure 2.1 there is the question of how the authority for meaning-making is ascribed: Who gets to decide what the words mean? For legal professionals, this is straightforwardly a question for the judicial member presiding over the case, potentially informed by past behaviours (case precedent). But for sociolinguists, this legal perspective can also be framed as a pragmatics problem: does the writer's intent (illocutionary force) outweigh the reader's understanding (perlocutionary effect) in deciding on the most legally meaningful interpretation? This question of 'who gets to decide' is critical to many types of communication, and is very often the cause of dispute in ordinary conversation. We should not be at all surprised to find that it arises in legal cases as well. However, as this case demonstrates, this aspect of interpreting the meaning of a legal text does not seem to be well articulated in the law. A case that exemplifies this unresolved conflict is the debate surrounding the political push to change Article 18C of the Racial Discrimination Act 1975 in Australia which reached the courts in the case of Eatock v Bolt.[1] At the heart of the debate was the question of whether Article 18C, which prohibits a person from making public comments that 'offend, insult, humiliate or intimidate…' the hearer, was in contravention of a person's right to free speech (McNamara & Quilter, 2014). In the course of the debate, those seeking to abolish 18C argued that it is not reasonable to ask a speaker[2] to anticipate whether or not a hearer might interpret what they produce as offensive (Gelber & McNamara, 2013). In pragmatic terms, the Act was promoting the hearer's interpretation (perlocutionary effect) over the speaker's intent (illocutionary force), and this was seen as untenable by those opposed to Article 18C (Aggarwal, 2012).

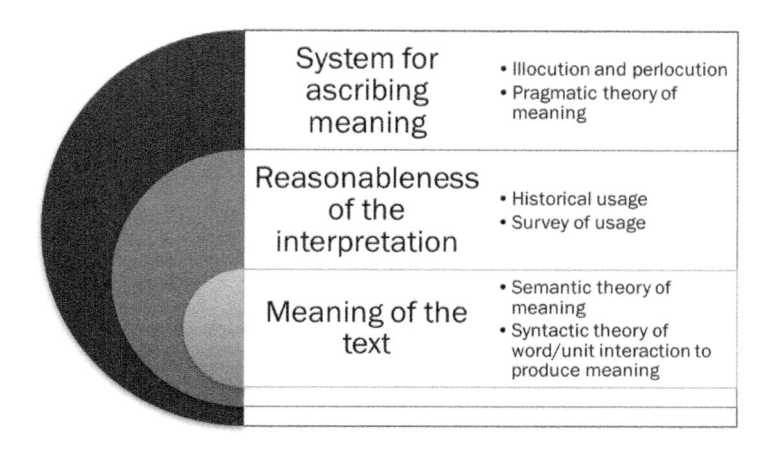

Figure 2.1 Diagram showing layers of analysis involved in a case to determine meaning in a legal text.

The pragmatic assumptions underlying the views of those opposed to 18C are consistent with the pragmatic assumptions of most judges in Australian courts and in other jurisdictions. According to Fiss '[a]djudication is interpretation: Adjudication is the process by which a judge comes to understand and express the meaning of an authoritative legal text and the values embodied in that text' (1981, p. 739) That is, the prevailing view seems to be that illocutionary force is more important than perlocutionary effect when it comes to identifying the authoritative meaning of a legal document such as a Court Order. The fact that the defendant might interpret the text to mean something other than the judge's intention is not a deciding factor. Yet, in insurance documents, for instance, it is by no means assured that illocutionary force is more important than perlocutionary effect. This is why such contracts begin with a long list of definitions that minimise the potential for misinterpretation and narrow the gap between illocutionary force and perlocutionary effect. And in the case of the Racial Discrimination Act in Australia, the debate was settled in favour of perlocutionary effect and Article 18C remains in the statutes. Overall, there is variability in how tension between these two forces is resolved, and a worthwhile avenue of future research might be a systematic pragmatic analysis of the data, including Court decisions, parliamentary debate and legal contracts.

At an intermediate level in Figure 2.1 there is the question of reasonableness: if the court is willing to accept that there can be a gap between what the judge intended and what the defendant understood by the text, then a test for reasonableness can demonstrate how much this gap needs to be taken into account. However, the findings of such research, including historical usage or current usage measured in surveys of the relevant data, will only be accepted if the court understands that such analysis is indeed the province of an expert linguist (Solan, 1998). Very often, questions of reasonableness are simply decided by the court as 'common sense' without any evidence one way or another (cf. Poirier, 1995). In the case study presented here, it was unclear whether the court held this view, or whether in fact the court did not allow that there might be a gap between the illocutionary force and the perlocutionary effect in the first place.

Finally, at the inner core of the problem is the semantic ambiguity itself. For linguists, this again seems to be a straightforwardly linguistic problem, which can be addressed with a systematic method of analysis based on theories of how language works (Aodha, 2017; Grice, 1975). This is a technical question, just like the technical question of what kind of instrument might have caused a fractured skull, and like the autopsy report, the linguistic report concerning the analysis of meaning can be regarded as expert and not common sense. However, again, because meaning-making is something all speakers do in everyday life, and believe they do accurately and consistently, it is difficult to convince a non-linguist that there is a theoretically sound approach to the analysis that can be applied with confidence and without relying on subjective speakers' opinions.

Perhaps by presenting the problem as having different layers, as in the previous diagram, it might be possible to demonstrate more easily the province and scope of linguistic expertise and how it intersects with judicial decision-making.

Applications to legal practice and procedures

The key issue that this case study addresses is whether or not a linguistic analysis of a legal text can contribute to a legal decision relating to the interpretation of that text. On the one hand, the problem can be framed as a semantic puzzle, solvable through the application of theory in a relatively simple analysis. Yet, the usual legal position on this response to the problem is that this is a question of identifying the author's intention in drafting the decision. An approach that clearly identifies the different layers of the problem shows that, in fact, these are questions to be resolved using different resources, and potentially, by different authorities. Research in this field could most usefully be directed towards establishing the relationship between the legal decision-making and the linguistic framing of the problem.

Final word

Retired Federal Court Judge, Peter Gray, has decided countless cases involving the interpretation of legal texts. As a student of linguistics, he also understands the linguistic problems that such interpretations involve. He considers that research is urgently needed that will address the problem of overlapping fields of expertise and 'territorial disputes' between linguists and lawyers. Indeed, he has explained to audiences of the International Association of Forensic Linguists that a fundamental difficulty for those of us presenting expert reports in courts is the confusion between the folk understanding of linguistics as merely some proficiency in language, and the professional or academic definition of linguistics as the scientific study of language, its structure and use. The sooner this gap can be closed, and lawyers introduced to the principles of linguistics or at least to its existence as a discipline, the easier it will be to resolve such territorial disputes and identify more easily which problems of meaning can be resolved by the courts and which might require the expertise acquired through study of linguistics.

Notes

1 [2011] FCA 1103.
2 Following conventions used in pragmatics research, I use *speaker* to cover all types of language producer including speakers, writers and signers, and the term *hearer* similarly covers all types of language receivers including hearers, readers and sign recipients.

References

Aggarwal, B. (2012). The Bolt case: Silencing speech or promoting tolerance. In H. Sykes, (Ed.) *More or less: Democracy and new media* (pp. 238–257). Melbourne: Future Leaders.

Aodha, M. M. (2017). New insights into the semantics of legal concepts and the legal dictionary. *International Journal of Speech, Language & the Law*, 24(2), 249–255. doi:10.1558/ijsll.34752

Bhatia, V. K. (1983). Simplification v. easification—the case of legal texts. *Applied Linguistics*, 4(1), 42–54.

Bhatia, V. K., Candlin, C. N., & Engberg, J. (2008). *Legal discourse across cultures and systems* (Vol. 1). Hong Kong: Hong Kong University Press.

Billmyer, K., & Varghese, M. (2000). Investigating instrument-based pragmatic variability: Effects of enhancing discourse completion tests. *Applied Linguistics, 21*(4), 517–552.

Félix-Brasdefer, J. C. (2010). Data collection methods in speech act performance. *Speech Act Performance: Theoretical, Empirical and Methodological Issues, 26*, 41.

Fiss, O. M. (1981). Objectivity and interpretation. *Stanford Law Review, 34*, 739.

Gelber, K., & McNamara, L. (2013). Freedom of speech and racial vilification in Australia: 'The Bolt case' in public discourse. *Australian Journal of Political Science, 48*(4), 470–484.

Grewendorf, G., & Rathert, M. (2009). *Formal linguistics and law* (vol. 212). Berlin: Walter de Gruyter.

Grice, H. P. (1975). Logic and conversation. In P. Cole & J. L. Morgan (Eds.), *Speech acts (syntax and semantics volume III)* (pp. 41–58). New York: Academic Press.

Kaplan, J. P. (2016). Case report: Elonis v. United States. *International Journal of Speech, Language & the Law, 23*(2), 275–292. doi:10.1558/ijsll.v23i2.29563

Kreidler, C.W. (1998). *Introducing English Semantics*. London: Routledge.

McNamara, L., & Quilter, J. (2014). Turning the spotlight on 'Offensiveness' as a basis for criminal liability. *Alternative Law Journal, 39*(1), 36–39.

Merkel, R., Krätzer, C., Hildebrandt, M., Kiltz, S., Kuhlmann, S., & Dittmann, J. (2016). A semantic framework for a better understanding, investigation and prevention of organized financial crime. In Meier, M., Reinhardt, D. & Wendzel, S. (Hrsg.), (Eds.), *Sicherheit 2016-Sicherheit, Schutz und Zuverlässigkeit* (pp. 55–66). Bonn: Gesellschaft für Informatik e.V.

Poirier, M. R. (1995). On whose authority: Linguistics' claim of expertise to interpret statutes. *Washington University Law Quarterly, 73*, 1025.

Solan, L. M. (1998). Linguistic experts as semantic tour guides. *Forensic Linguistics: The International Journal of Speech, Language and the Law, 5*(2), 87–106.

Part II
Police procedures

3 Police interviewing

Questioning strategies in UK and US models of training[1]

Introduction

Since the 1990s when I began my study of police institutional discourse, the contributions of linguists to police interviewing practice have changed considerably. At the time that I was publishing a paper on police training interviews with children in Victoria, Australia (Heydon, 1997), there were few linguists publishing research about police interviewing. The language of police interviewing was being directly addressed by Roger Shuy in the United States (Shuy, 1998) and John Gibbons in Australia (Gibbons, 1996) but for the most part, forensic linguists were focusing on courtroom language or the language practices in the justice system more broadly (Cooke, 1996; Coulthard, 1997; Kaplan, Green, Cunningham, & Levi, 1995; Levi, 1994; Solan, 1998; Woolls & Coulthard, 1998). In particular, linguists were not represented amongst the ranks of academic researchers who, in the 1990s, were re-shaping the way that police in England and Wales were conducting investigative interviews (Clarke & Milne, 2001; Milne & Bull, 1999; Pearse & Gudjonsson, 1996; Shepherd, 1993; Stephenson & Moston, 1993). This is important because that program of change, arising from the Philips Commission Report UK (1981) and the subsequent Police and Criminal Evidence Act UK (1984), represents the most significant and far-reaching development in investigative interviewing in the last four decades (Clarke & Milne, 2001). The impact of these changes has been felt in many countries where police academies have implemented investigative interviewing training models based on the transformations led by the Home Office in the UK (Heydon, 2012; Schollum, 2005; Snook & Keating, 2011; Westera, Kebbell, & Milne, 2011). The initial empirical basis for this wave of interviewing reform drew only on research from psychology, particularly cognitive psychology relating to eyewitness memory (Geiselman, Fisher, MacKinnon, & Holland, 1986; Kebbell, 1997; Powell & Thomson, 1994). Despite there being an extensive body of research in discourse analysis, pragmatics and interactional sociolinguistics, linguists were not involved in the early stages of development of the dominant model of interviewing training in England and Wales, known as the PEACE model (Clarke & Milne, 2001). The linguistic research that was relevant to police interviewing practices, including my own early work, did not engage directly with existing or emerging models of training, but rather focused on responding to linguistic problems and extending our knowledge of 'how people do things with words' (Auburn, Drake, & Willig, 1995; Heydon, 2005b; Johnson, 2008). Notable exceptions are Janet Ainsworth's work on the Miranda warning (Ainsworth, 1993) and Roger Shuy's work on police language (Shuy, 1998), but these academics were focused on issues arising in the United States and were not contributing to the development of new interviewing models taking place in the United Kingdom. It took some time before linguists began to re-frame their research into the language of police interviewing so that it could address questions about police practices in addition to addressing questions about discourse practices. Since then, a number of studies have addressed various aspects of police interviewing language, especially questioning practices and the legal requirement to negotiate suspects' rights, e.g. the Miranda rights in the United States, or the right to silence in Australia and the United Kingdom (Ehrlich, Eades, & Ainsworth, 2016; Mason, 2013). These studies are more likely to be framed with reference to existing interviewing methods and principles and, as such, have more relevance for police practitioners. While not all linguistic research into police interviewing needs to be overtly aligned with police goals, it is still important, in my view, that researchers interested in this field are at least aware of the empirical and theoretical research that currently underpins police models of interviewing. Apart from making our research more relevant and disseminating our findings more widely, police interviewing specialists are very interested in what linguists have to offer, in particular anything that can help to identify suitable approaches to questioning or means by which interviewee's responses can be analysed (Oxburgh, 2016). This chapter will demonstrate how to analyse the language of police interviews in the context of existing models of training such as the PEACE model extensively used in the United Kingdom, Norway, New Zealand and parts of Australia and Canada.

In addition to the PEACE model, there is a second popular method of interviewing, known as the Reid method, which is the dominant training method in the United States and Canada (Buckley, 2006). Until the reform process began in the United Kingdom, the Reid method was used as the basis for interviewing training in many countries, including Australia, even though several of its techniques are not permitted under Australian law. Nonetheless the legacy of the Reid method lives on in many countries around the world, even where the PEACE model has been introduced. This is in part because detective training schools and individual officers sometimes avail themselves of training courses based on Reid method interviewing which are offered commercially by some US law enforcement agencies as well as private training providers. The potential for officers to be exposed to conflicting principles and practices between the PEACE model and the Reid model does not seem to be well understood, and so following the presentation of an analytic approach to police interview discourse, this chapter will proceed to a demonstration of how those analytical methods can highlight the key differences between the two approaches.

I assume some familiarity with each method, and so for those completely new to this field, I recommend Milne and Bull (1999) for an introduction to the cognitive approach to investigative interviewing used in the United Kingdom and Buckley (2006) for an introduction to the Reid technique.

Approach to the problem

Although the nine-step interrogation stage of the Reid method of interviewing used in North America has attracted a great deal of criticism and commentary from a variety of academics and practitioners, there are few published studies that provide a systematic *linguistic* analysis of the interrogation techniques suggested (Shuy, 1998). Snook, Eastwood, Stinson, Tedeschini, and House (2010) subject the Reid techniques to scrutiny from a psychological perspective, especially the reliance on behavioural indicators of deception and the intense focus on seeking a confession, and support the use of cognitive interviewing (Fisher, Geiselman, & Amador, 1989) or other information seeking approaches instead. Such a systematic comparison of the Reid method to the cognitive interviewing approach (e.g. PEACE, ECI or investigative interviewing) has not yet been conducted using linguistic theories and frameworks of analysis, and it seems timely that such an attempt should be made. This chapter therefore compares the discourse and interactional structures of the cognitive interviewing method, an evidence-based model for best-practice investigative interviewing (Clarke & Milne, 2001), with the linguistic features of the Reid technique, as it is represented in the literature (Inbau, Reid, Buckley, & Jayne, 2011). Claims made by the authors of the Reid method about the efficacy of several specific language strategies are subjected to linguistic analysis in order to ascertain first whether they are based on sound linguistic theory and research findings, and second how they compare to the techniques used in cognitive interviewing.

Identifying research questions

In order to conduct a research project that focuses on the discourse of police interviewing, it is important that the research questions are framed according to the goals of the project. This book is intended for researchers who are interested in the application of linguistic analysis to justice contexts, so I am therefore going to assume that the main purpose of the reader's police interviewing research is to apply the findings to policy or practice in justice institutions. In this chapter, I will be framing a discourse analysis of police interviewing in relation to the two main training and interviewing methods used internationally. This analysis forms part of a larger project that aims to inform decision-making in law enforcement institutions about interviewing methods and training. Therefore, the main research question responds to an issue arising from the current training environment of police interviewing around the world, namely the compatibility of the two main training methods.

Main research question:

> Are the approaches to questioning used in Reid method police interviewing compatible with the approaches to questioning used in the cognitive interviewing methods of police interviewing?

Given that the analysis is based on linguistic tools, the main research question must be supported by sub-questions that are answerable by linguistic analysis.

Sub-questions:

> What are the linguistic characteristics of questioning in each method?
> What are the policing goals of questioning in each method?
> Can the linguistic characteristics of questioning in one method achieve the policing goals of the other method?

Data analysis

In the tradition of Harvey Sacks, the pioneer of Conversation Analysis (CA), I am going to begin the analysis with a data extract (Sacks, 1992). This police interview excerpt (Excerpt 3.1) is from an analysis that I provided in Heydon (2005b).

In this example from an Australian police interview with a suspect, the police interviewer POL1 elicits a narrative response from the suspect SPT1. The original analysis showed how, in fact, the suspect offers a narrative that precisely matches the officer's request, and is therefore far from ideal. A 'free narrative' would take the officer's question as a starting point and continue until all relevant and available information had been offered. In this case, the suspect had

Excerpt 3.1 Extract from a police interview with a suspect (INT1) recorded in Victoria, Australia

68.	POL1:	(0.5) right (1.9) w'l (0.8) y' how co- can you start Friday
69.		what di- (0.3) what started (0.4) on Friday
70.	SPT1:	well (0.3) what started Friday was Friday morning when
71.		I received a phone call
72.		(1.6) n that was around ten (0.2) yeah (0.4) ten to ten thirty
73.		cause it was (0.4) not far after the news
74.		(1.3) so I picked it up answered and they said
75.		(0.3) Joh- ah Johnny? Johnny
76.		(0.6) I said yeah (0.5) speaking
77.		(1.2) they said right if you go anywhere near the shop (0.6) cr any where near the house
78.		(0.8) you're going to get your legs broken
79.		(1.1) and that was it
80.		(0.2) just hanged up

previously begun such a free-ranging narrative earlier in the interview but been cut off twice in rapid succession by the police officer and so restrains himself to an answer that fits within the scope of the officer's question. Further questions and prompts are required to elicit the long and complicated story from the suspect, and the police officer never quite regains the level of cooperation that the suspect displayed at the start of the interview. In other words, the suspect appears to be struggling to find the appropriate set of conversational norms to apply in this situation: he first tried to tell a story, but the officer seemed to want specific details clarified, and so now, wary of the officer's propensity to interrupt, he answers cautiously and limits the topic of his response more precisely to her question. This, together with many other examples from the data set of 12 police interviews, demonstrates that suspects work surprisingly hard to balance constraints of pragmatic rules of conversation with the institutionally imposed rules of the interview.

I am going to use this extract and further extracts presented below to demonstrate two tools that can be used to analyse police interview discourse. These analyses are intended to contribute to the body of knowledge about interviewing practice but I believe that they also make a useful contribution to the field of discourse analysis. In particular, this approach highlights the difficulties that are encountered by lay speakers when they encounter an institutional discourse event and try to apply normative rules of conversation to the interaction with the professional speaker, as in Excerpt 3.1.

The first tool – participation frameworks

By far one of the most useful findings to come out of my discourse analysis approach to police interviewing data has been the importance of topic management and how it affects voluntary confessions (Heydon, 2012). But to analyse topic management in police interviews, I want to first introduce another tool: Goffman's participant roles (Goffman, 1974; Levinson, 1988).

Taking an approach that draws on interactional sociolinguistics, participant role analysis demonstrates how speakers align to various roles in their spoken interactions. Roles are distributed between participants through their co-constructed conversation, such that speakers align to different aspects of speech production at different times, according to their self-perception in relation to what they are saying. This is much better understood through an example.

The extract we have already seen shows a reasonably straightforward example of someone telling a story. The suspect, following a prompt, relates the story of what happened to him one morning at home. We can describe his alignment to the story according to three participant roles: animator, author and principal (Goffman, 1981). He is the animator of the story – he is physically producing the words using his voice box. He is the author of the story – he is choosing the words he will say and the order in which he will say them. And finally, he is the principal

46 *Police procedures*

Excerpt 3.2 Extract from a police interview with a suspect (INT2) recorded in Victoria, Australia

230.	pio2:	all right↓* well when you had hold of her bicep⇒
231.		(.) which↓ (0.2) arm was that do you remember↑
232.	SPT2:	(0.4) yip↑
233.	pio2:	(0.4) which one↓
234.	SPT2:	(0.2) right one∧
235.	pio2:	(0.2) a::hm↓ at some stage⇒
236.		didja have ever have hold of 'er other arm↑
237.		(0.6) bicep∧
238.	SPT2:	(1.0) no∧ I↓ (0.4) no∧
239.	pio2:	a::hm⇒ (2.0) it's a::h⇒ (.) she's had (.) some injuries on 'er arm⇒
240.		(0.2) bruising to bo:th (.) biceps↓
241.	SPT2:	mm hm∧=
242.	pio2:	=at some stage↓ (0.2) didju have hold of 'er other bicep↑
243.		(.) dragging her outside↑
244.		((sound of door closing⇒ or seat moving))
245.	SPT2:	(1.4) not that I can remember⇒
246.	pio2:	so you can't explain⇒ how those⇒ (.) marks would 'ave got there↑
247.	SPT2:	(0.4) the one on the right (.) arm∧ would have been from me⇒// *grabbin a∧ (.) but↓
248.	pio2:	right* (4.4) and⇒ OK⇒ u:m⇒
249.		(1.0) after the second⇒ (0.2) time you've (0.2) grabbed a∧
250.		(0.6) you went back inside∧
251.		what happened then↓

of the story – he takes responsibility for the impact that the story might have on the world. Although in ordinary conversation this role alignment is normal, there are other possible configurations of the participant roles in a police interview. This is demonstrated in Excerpt 3.2.

What we see here is a different role alignment. In lines 235–240, the police officer is forced to ask a question and then add further information that he had clearly intended for the suspect to produce. We can say that this information about 'bruising to both biceps' is definitely not produced by the suspect: the police officer is the animator. The suspect also did not write the words of the utterance: the police officer is the author. But what is interesting is the role of principal. Line 246 in Excerpt 3.2 suggests that the police officer is avoiding the role of principal of this utterance and instead is trying to shift this alignment onto the suspect, asking him to explain the bruising. There are more obvious examples of this, such as the one given in Excerpt 3.3.

Excerpt 3.3 Extract from a police interviewing with a suspect (INT2) recorded in Victoria, Australia

198.	pio2:	(1.0) w' would you agree that ⇒
199.		thas: (0.4) not the normal way that anyone would ah⇒
200.		(0.2) assist someone up⇒ onto their feet by pick'n them up by the hair∧

'Would you agree that' is often heard in police interviews of this period in Australia. To me, it signals a weakening of the impact of the interview evidence because the police officer has been unable to create a conversational environment in which the suspect is able to contribute information with the three-role framework, which I have dubbed S3R: suspect (takes up) three roles. Instead, the officer is taking up the two roles of animator and author (2 As) and trying to persuade the suspect to take up the principal role, thus creating a confession by proxy. I called this P2RA: police (takes up) 2 A roles (author + animator) (Heydon, 2005a, 2005b).

Role analysis such as this can usefully distinguish between high value evidentiary contributions from the suspect (S3R) and low value evidentiary contributions (P2RA). This is especially useful to prosecutors who need to identify weaknesses in the police interview evidence, but it also has investigative value, because stretches of P2RA turns will highlight areas that might require further corroboration, while S3R turns might provide more valuable and reliable leads in a case.

The second tool – topic management in CA

CA provides the capacity to track the ways in which participants in spoken interaction introduce, maintain or shift topics (Button & Casey, 1984; Jefferson, 1984). In casual conversation, it is usual for participants to change topics at will, often by responding first to the topic of their interlocutor, and then using some connecting remarks to establish a new topic (Button & Casey, 1984). Whose topic gets maintained and whose gets ignored is a fascinating study in power and status in conversations, but these patterns occur within a normative set of rules that allow anyone to change topics within certain parameters (don't interrupt, don't change topics abruptly and so on) (Schegloff, 1968). Interviews are different. I have shown elsewhere that police interviews follow the chain rule of question and answer adjacency pairs that Frankel (1990) described in medical interviews. That is, all the first pair parts (questions) are allocated to the interviewer and all the second pair parts (answers) are allocated to the interviewee. Even if there is a disruption to this sequence, such as a clarification question from the suspect, this is dealt with as an insert sequence (Jefferson, 1972; Sacks, Schegloff, & Jefferson, 1974), and the chain rule resumes.

One of the notable features of an answer is that it must be topically relevant to the preceding first pair part question (Sacks et al., 1974). If during a conference presentation, I say to the chair, 'how much time do I have left?' and she says 'bananas are yellow,' then that doesn't function as an answer to my question. If a police officer asks: 'What did you do then?' and the suspect answers 'My ex-wife and I get along very well thank you' then that is also not functioning as an answer to the question. But if this information about his ex-wife is critical to the suspect's narrative, how can he include it in his response when he has not been asked a question on that topic? The following extract from INT1 shows how SPT1 manages this problem (Excerpt 3.4):

48 *Police procedures*

Excerpt 3.4 Extract from a police interview with a suspect (INT1) recorded in Victoria, Australia

87.	pio1:	so wadcha do then↓
88.	SPT1:	(0.5) w'l (1.1) made meself another cup of coffee⇒
89.		and I just thought about it∧
90.		and I said what's going on⇒
91.		this can't be right↑
92.		(1.0) s- Betty and I are getting on all right∧
93.		I don't go anywhere near their house unless I phone∧
94.		(1.8) I ring her I say can I go and get this and go and get that∧
95.		she says yep∧ no worries∧
96.		and a (0.2) few times she said you don't have to phone to go around ere⇒
97.		you just go around and get what you∧ want⇒
98.		(1.8) and (0.4) I go to the shop there a couple aw
99.		(0.3) every second day or third day
100.		(0.8) and get milk bread and a few vegies and that that I need∧
101.		(1.1) and smokes∧
102.		and we get on all right just as friends ⇒
103.		like we bump into each other in the street⇒
104.		(0.5) //best of* friends∧
105.	pio1:	thi-* this phone call happened at ten-thirty in the morning↓
106.	SPT1:	(0.4) bout ten ten-thirty in the morning↓

In ordinary conversation this might be seen as rambling, but would otherwise be treated as a legitimate attempt to change topics using a stepwise topic transition. In CA Harvey Sacks (Sacks, 1987) and later Gail Jefferson (Jefferson, 1988) established two main types of topic shift device: the stepwise topic transition which SPT1 produces here, and the disjunctive topic shift, which is rarely seen unmarked in ordinary conversation but which POL1 produces in line 105. In fact, she produces this topic shift unmarked and in overlap to interrupt SPT1's narrative.

Despite the potentially adversarial nature of police interviews with suspects, this kind of topic-shifting behaviour is still problematic, because the chain rule (Frankel, 1990) means that suspects can only answer questions, and the Gricean maxim of relation (Grice, 1975) means that their answers have to be topically relevant to the question. The upshot is that the only way that suspects can introduce a new topic is by using a stepwise topic transition during their response to a question. Literally, the only way that a suspect can volunteer information and produce statements using the S3R participation framework is by not answering the question.

To summarise, this analysis has demonstrated how to use two linguistic tools by applying them to the turn-taking of suspects and police officers in actual police interviews. The data were selected from an old data set of Australian police interviews which were conducted by low-ranking officers with no specialised interviewing training. This was useful because they included a range of approaches to questioning and topic management, rather than being confined to a specific approach based on a specialised technique. This analysis established that the participant role alignment labelled S3R, where the suspect took up the three roles of author, animator and principal of the narrative turns, was associated with a version of events relatively uncontaminated by the police version. The analysis of topic management demonstrated that the constraints of turn-taking in the interview format forces suspects to rely on stepwise topic transitions to introduce new information, and that this is only possible if suspects are given an opportunity to talk freely and move away from the topic of the question.

Interpreting data

Cognitive interviewing methods

The problem of using a question-answer format to elicit reliable information from suspects is well understood in the scientific literature that underpins the so-called Cognitive Interview or PEACE training model in England and Wales (Bull & Milne, 2004; Milne & Bull, 1999; Snook, Luther, Quinlan, & Milne, 2012). Closed questions that elicit a limited range of possible answers are regarded as last resort options (Griffiths & Milne, 2006). Information seeking must commence with an open-ended prompt, a TED question like 'Tell me everything that happened on Friday night, *even the little things that you think are not important.*' The second part (in italics) is designed to counter among other things the pragmatic rules that usually prevent speakers from producing highly detailed descriptions in response to questions in ordinary conversation. There is a strong emphasis on the elicitation of a free narrative at the start of the interview, and at any point where new information is sought. All possible effort must be made to encourage the suspect to tell their own story in their own words before probing questions are used to clarify the details and prepare for the strategic presentation of evidence (Bull & Milne, 2004; Griffiths & Milne, 2006).

Using the terminology of participant role analysis presented above, the elicitation of a free narrative using open questions or prompts maximises the opportunity for suspects to produce statements in the S3R participation framework. When information is provided by the suspects in this way, it is much more valuable as evidence in court, and it is more reliable because it is relatively uncontaminated by the interviewer's own biases.

We now turn to the consideration of policing goals, as set out in earlier research sub-question (b). The policing goals that underpin the training in England and Wales are clearly identified in a set of principles (College of Policing UK, 2018). The College of Policing presentation of the Principles does not discuss truth seeking except in passing but rather focuses on reliability and probity. Broadly speaking, the goals of the interview can be defined in England and Wales as respecting the rights of the interviewee, gathering information that is of high quality, unbiased and reliable, and following due process (see Chapter 4 for a complete list of the principles). This is appropriately supported by the use of an evidence-based method of interviewing that minimises police contamination of the evidence and focuses on reliable narrative turns. Linguistically, this manifests as the use of open questions or prompts to elicit long S3R turns from the suspect which might include stepwise topic transitions away from topic of the original question.

The Reid method

The Reid method uses two phases of questioning suspects: the behavioural analysis interview (BAI) and the nine-step interrogation. According to the literature, the BAI is intended to be non-accusatory and information gathering. However, it differs from the Cognitive Interview in several important ways. First of all, it is used to eliminate persons not believed to be guilty in order that anyone else will be subjected to the interrogation process. This is a very different process from English law, where suspects are cautioned[2] and interviewed accordingly from the beginning while witnesses are not cautioned and are interviewed using a different set of techniques (though both suspect and witness interviews are based on the same principles of open, non-biased investigation).

While the Reid training guidelines discuss the importance of eliciting information from the interviewee, the literature makes it very clear that the main purpose of the Reid method interview is to identify guilt, and the kind of information that is being sought is the information that will point to the suspect's guilty conscience or deceptive behaviour. This framing of the interview as a credibility test is made abundantly clear in a 2008 article promoting the BAI which opens with the line: 'Everyone lies to the police' (Horvath, Blair, & Buckley, 2008). The article then goes on to describe the most important types of questions to use in the interview and their function in eliciting very specific types of responses.

These questions are reproduced in the following format that they are presented in the article (Excerpt 3.5).

Excerpt 3.5 From Horvath et al. (2008: 107)

I: (Purpose) Andy, what is your understanding of the purpose of this interview with me today?

S: (Innocent) Well, last Sunday morning when the bookkeeping department was counting up the deposits they found that the $3,200 deposit from the men's department was missing and I know that I put it in the safe. So the reason I am here is to prove that I didn't steal it.

S: (Guilty) Well, I guess they may have misplaced a deposit envelope and I'm just here to help them find out what might have happened to it.

I: (Attitude) How do you feel about being interviewed concerning this missing deposit?

S: (Innocent) Oh, I don't mind at all. I want to prove to them that I didn't steal it and hopefully through these interviews they will be able to catch the thief.

S: (Guilty) I don't feel one way or the other. It's something that I have to do to keep my job.

I: (Bait) Andy, something you may not be aware of is that most drop safes have a counting mechanism on the underside of the drop slot. Very simply the

> force of an envelope entering the safe causes the counter to advance in increments of one. Now if you in fact did put that envelope in the safe last Saturday the counter should read 11, because that's the total number of envelopes that should have been dropped. Now I don't know if this particular safe is equipped with that mechanism, but if it is, can you think of any reason why the counter would indicate 10 drops instead of 11?
> S: (Innocent) If it does it's not from my envelope because I know for sure I put that envelope in the safe.
> (Guilty) Gee . . ., I don't know very much about mechanical things, maybe it got stuck or something.

As can be seen in Excerpt 3.5, each of the sample questions includes two sample responses, and the assumption is that all responses can be categorised as either indicating guilt or innocence. There seems to be relatively little emphasis on eliciting new information or ensuring that the questioning strategy will avoid contamination of the evidence by the police interviewer. Although these are not authentic data and this commentary by no means constitutes an exhaustive analysis of the BAI method, I chose these examples because they were published in a paper that is intended to provide a description of the method sufficiently detailed that other researchers can use it as the basis for their own investigation of the efficacy of the BAI. The authors of the article, who have also published many of the training materials produced by the Reid organisation, state that 'this article is intended to present an overview of the BAI and the research which supports it so that practitioners and researchers will not be misled by findings that have little, if any, ecological validity' (Horvath et al., 2008, p. 102). It is pertinent to note that the authors are defending the BAI method in light of findings from a study by Vrij, Mann, and Fisher (2006) which they, the authors, claim lacks ecological validity and 'demonstrated significant misunderstandings of the development, structure and research regarding the BAI' (Horvath et al., 2008, p. 102).

In light of this, we shall take the questions presented in the article as our data and analyse their structure and function from a linguistic perspective. First, it is notable that they are very specific, and designed to elicit a very narrow range of responses. For instance, the first question requests specific information (the interviewee's understanding of the purpose of the interview) and does not suggest to the interviewee that they can elaborate or provide additional detail in their response beyond the topic of 'the purpose of the interview.' As a prompt for a narrative, it is indirect and opaque. That is, one interpretation of the question is that 'the purpose of the interview' is the actions taken by the interviewee relating to a theft. The sample responses assume that this is the interpretation that the interviewee will apply. However, there are other possible interpretations such as a focus on the actions of the interviewer (e.g. the purpose of the interview is for the interviewer to ask some questions about a theft) or a focus on the goals of the employer[3] (e.g. the purpose of the interview is for the employer to find out who stole the money). The question itself does not indicate which of these interpretations is intended so there is no certainty that it will function as illustrated by the sample responses. Even if the interviewee did produce one of these responses, the function of the question is not explained to the interviewee. Indeed, the strategy behind the questioning rests on the interviewee remaining ignorant of the interviewer's true purpose in asking these questions. More broadly, the purpose of the interview as a 'behavioural analysis' needs to be hidden from interviewees or it cannot function as intended. This reveals a contrast with the cognitive interviewing models where explaining the purpose of the interview is central to the elicitation of more detailed and more reliable responses (Fisher et al., 1989; Geiselman et al., 1986; Vrij, Hope, & Fisher, 2014).

The other sample questions can be analysed in much the same way: each question requests specific information and the third question relies on a long descriptive turn by the investigator followed by a highly specific question. This can be characterised as a P2RA elicitation, where the investigator provides the bulk of the information and seeks a confirmation from the interviewee. There are some instances where such a strategy might be used as part of a cognitive interviewing method such as in the strategic use of evidence (SUE) approach. However, the purpose of SUE is not to identify behavioural characteristics from the responses, but rather to reveal the evidence held by the investigator strategically so as to maximise its value in the questioning (Hartwig, Granhag, & Luke, 2014). Moreover, there is no indication that the investigator is providing factual information in the 'Bait' question used for the BAI.

The analysis of the question-answer turns in the BAI suggests that officers are being taught that their questioning strategy in the interview needs to be designed to elicit only the responses that will help them to sort the guilty from the innocent, and not to encourage broad and unexpected responses. In terms of the discourse structure, we can observe that the BAI method does not seek to maximise free narrative responses from the interviewee, and does not 'hand over control' to the interviewee, which is encouraged in the cognitive interviewing training manuals. There are few opportunities in this style of questioning for a suspect to elaborate on a response to the extent that he or she can introduce new information voluntarily, i.e. take up an S3R position in relation to new information. This is because any stepwise topic transition is highly likely to flout the Gricean maxim of relation by being unrelated to the (very specific) question.

Our research sub-questions set out three problems to consider in order to answer the main question of whether or not the two different interviewing methods practised in the United Kingdom and the United States are compatible:

a   What are the linguistic characteristics of questioning in each method?
b   What are the policing goals of questioning in each method?
c   Can the linguistic characteristics of questioning in one method achieve the policing goals of the other method?

The first problem was the identification of the linguistic characteristics of each method. In the analysis presented here, we focused on the use of participant role alignments and topic management tools to distinguish between different approaches to questioning. According to the cognitive interviewing methods, interviews are characterised by open-ended questions or prompts that elicit free narratives in the S3R participation framework. We could also see that these interviews are more likely to be characterised by the inclusion of stepwise topic shifts by suspects, because of the emphasis on suspect-controlled narrative responses where the topic can move away from the original topic of the question. Moreover, the use of open, non-specific prompts encourages suspects to provide whatever information they find relevant, rather than only the information that the investigator finds relevant. Investigators can follow the suspect-led narrative responses with probing questions and the strategic presentation of evidence to elicit responses to the police topics without contaminating the suspect's own version of events.

The Reid method BAI is characterised by closed questions that have a specific purpose. This can include questions in the P2RA framework. There is not an emphasis on the interviewee providing information in the S3R framework, and the narrowly defined questions do not have, as their main purpose, the elicitation of wide-ranging information from the interviewee. Thus interviewees are unlikely to produce stepwise topic transitions to provide new information in the BAI.

The goals of each of these interviewing methods are also substantially different: the goals of the Cognitive Interview are to elicit reliable and detailed information, follow due process and treat the interviewee fairly. The Reid method BAI is intended to test for behavioural characteristics that might indicate deception or guilt. The assessment of the interviewee's guilt is used to justify the application of the nine-step interrogation technique, which aims to apply maximum pressure to elicit a confession.

Finally, we arrive at the third problem: can the linguistic characteristics of questioning in one method be applied to achieve the goals of the other method. The analysis suggests that this is not possible. First, the policing goals of cognitive interviewing methods require information from suspects that is reliable and uncontaminated. This cannot be achieved using probing questions framed by P2RA participant role alignments. Similarly, questions that are narrowly defined, as in the BAI, will not maximise the opportunity for voluntarily produced information through stepwise topic transitions. However, the behavioural analysis that is the goal of the Reid method interview arguably could be better achieved using open-ended prompts than the narrow 'trick' questions that are suggested. This is because, according to the literature on lie detection, the only reliable way to assess credibility through questioning is to elicit highly detailed responses and use the detail to compare the suspect's version of events to hard evidence or to identify inconsistencies in their story (Hartwig et al., 2014; Vrij, Granhag, Mann, & Leal, 2011). Therefore, if the goal of the Reid method interview is to sort the truth-tellers from the liars, then the best approach is one that prioritises long S3R turns with maximum opportunity for volunteering information through stepwise topic transitions such as the cognitive interviewing method.

Applications to legal practice and procedures

This brief comparative analysis is intended to indicate how existing forms of discourse analysis and sociolinguistics can be applied to police interviewing. This is an important area of research that needs more attention because according to commentators from a range of disciplines, the Reid method police interviewing training used across the United States is deeply problematic (Heydon, 2002; Meissner & Kassin, 2004; Shuy, 1998; Snook et al., 2010; Vrij et al., 2006; Williams, 2000). For those who are satisfied that the US constitution or governance structures provide sufficient protection from any coercive behaviour by the police, there still remains the issue of how the Reid method is being implemented in countries which have no such protections, and quasi-militarised police forces. Even in countries that have officially moved towards cognitive interviewing models and ethical questioning, there is still commercial training available in Reid method tools such as the BAI and other 'lie detection' techniques. Companies offering such training in Australia, for instance, identify state and federal law enforcement bodies as clients (Australian Polygraph Services, nd), even though most Australian police academies have adopted cognitive interviewing methods for their basic training and for specialist units (Hill & Moston, 2011; Wright & Powell, 2007). As mentioned in the introduction to this chapter, this means that some Australian police officers are being taught cognitive interviewing in the academy and then seeking private training in Reid method tools.[4] This leads to a situation where the two methods are most likely being applied side by side, whereas what we have shown in the analysis here is that they are inherently incompatible.

In the United States, recent negative publicity around the Reid method following the Making A Murderer television series (Ricciardi & Demos, 2015) has caused some training organisations to move away from coercive interrogation styles (Hager, 2017) and in Canada, where the Reid method has similarly dominated the market, researchers and police have been advocating for a shift to non-coercive investigative approaches to interviewing for some years (Snook et al., 2010; Snook, House, MacDonald, & Eastwood, 2012; Snook & Keating, 2011). China too is experiencing a shift away from coercive techniques (Yuan, 2010) and Indonesia is another example of a country where cognitive interviewing is being introduced (Goodman-Delahunty & Howes, 2014; Muniroh & Aziz, 2016).

Given these changes in practice around the world, it is more important than ever that practitioners understand the differences between these two methods. As we have demonstrated, trying to achieve the goals of the Cognitive Interview, or any investigative interviewing approach, using the Reid method tools will be counterproductive. For those countries moving away from Reid, this research does provide some cause for optimism since the goals of a Reid method interview can still be achieved using tools developed for cognitive interviewing.

Finally, it is clear to me that investigative interviewing methods are conspicuously absent from legal training, especially undergraduate law degrees. Some lawyer-client communication skills are usually discussed by lecturers, but law students are rarely provided with a systematic approach to eliciting reliable information from clients, nor are they given any insight into the interviewing methods that their clients are subjected to by police and other authorities. As far as I can see, lawyers are ill-equipped to detect poor police interviewing practices nor raise an objection to such practices when they occur. While this chapter has dealt primarily with a comparative analysis of the two main methods, the tools used to evaluate the reliability of participant contributions (e.g. S3R and P2RA frameworks) could easily be applied by defence lawyers seeking to identify potential weaknesses in the interview evidence produced by the prosecution.

Final word

Emeritus Professor Roger Shuy has contributed substantially to the linguistic analysis of police interviewing over many decades. Indeed, I can still recall my excitement as a research student when I came across his book *The language of confession, interrogation, and deception* (Shuy, 1998) and brought it in to my supervisor to reassure her that I was on the right track in pursuing this topic in my PhD. I will leave the final word on this subject to him:

> The police interview is a specific type of speech event in which police officers have all the conversational power to ask the questions and gather information by eliciting facts and challenging omissions and inaccuracies before accusing and trying to elicit a confession. Linguistic analysis can help with problems in ways the police present the legally required warning, conduct the interview, and present their evidence at trial.
>
> Successful interviewers begin with open-ended questions in the hope that suspects will implicate themselves. Less successful interviewers shortcut the interview by leaping directly into accusations. Even less successful interviews contain evidence of coercion, which most alert defence attorneys should notice. In the United States, police are permitted to use certain types of deception, including untruths that they already have information to entice the suspect to confess such as the alleged existence of DNA evidence, fingerprints, or that other co-conspirators have already confessed.
>
> Often unnoticed are other ways that police interviewers either intentionally or unintentionally use language that contains deceptive ambiguity (Shuy, 2017).They can confuse suspects with sudden topic switching, by using indirect speech acts that vaguely hint at what the police want to hear, by concealing or omitting important information, by minimizing the illegality of the alleged crime, by blocking the suspects' efforts to present their own topics, by using conversational strategies such as interrupting to block what the suspects are trying to say and perhaps most of all by using ambiguity in the words and phrases of their questions, especially with unclear grammatical referencing of pronouns like 'you,' 'it' and 'they,' which can be understood in more than one way. More blatant deception occurs when only a signed confession statement is presented as evidence instead of the entire police interview from which that confession was derived.
>
> The contributions of linguists can be helpful whenever police interviews are presented as evidence in criminal cases.
>
> Roger W. Shuy
Distinguished Professor of Linguistics, Emeritus
Georgetown University

Notes

1 I wish to thank Professor Roger Shuy for his helpful and erudite feedback on earlier drafts of this chapter.
2 'Cautioned' in this context means that the police interviewer ensures that the suspect understands that they are being interviewed as a suspect and that they may therefore exercise certain legal rights such as the right not to answer questions and the right to communicate with a legal representative.
3 These are workplace investigations rather than police investigations.
4 Anecdotal reports from the Victoria Police Detective Training School, for example, suggest that detectives seek Reid method training from agencies in the United States, or have training delivered locally by visiting Reid method proponents such as officers from the Royal Canadian Mounted Police. There is not a suggestion that such training has an official place in the curriculum of the DTS.

References

Ainsworth, J. (1993). In a different register: The pragmatics of powerlessness in police interrogation. *Yale Law Journal*, 103, 259–322.
Auburn, T., Drake, S., & Willig, C. (1995). 'You punched him, didn't you?': Versions of violence in accusatory interviews. *Discourse and Society*, 6(3), 353–386.
Australian Polygraph Services. (nd). About us. Retrieved from http://polygraph.com.au/about-us/
Buckley, J. P. (2006). The Reid technique of interviewing and interrogation. In T. Williamson (Ed.), *Investigative interviewing: Rights, research and regulation* (pp. 190–206). Cullompton: Willan.
Bull, R., & Milne, B. (2004). Attempts to improve the police interviewing of suspects. In G. D. Lassiter (Ed.), *Interrogations, confessions, and entrapment* (pp. 181–196). New York: Kluwer Academic.
Button, G., & Casey, N. (1984). Generating topic: The use of topic initial elicitors. In J. M. Atkinson & J. Heritage (Eds.), *Structures of social action: Studies in conversation analysis* (pp. 167–190). Cambridge: Cambridge University Press.
Clarke, C., & Milne, R. (2001). *National evaluation of the PEACE investigative interviewing course* (PRAS no. 149). London: Home Office.
College of Policing UK. (2018). Investigative interviewing: Principles and ethics. Retrieved from https://www.app.college.police.uk/app-content/investigations/investigative-interviewing/-principles-and-ethics
Cooke, M. (1996). A different story: Narrative versus 'question and answer' in Aboriginal evidence. *Forensic Linguistics: The International Journal of Speech, Language and the Law*, 3(2), 273–288.
Coulthard, M. (1997). A failed appeal. *Forensic Linguistics: The International Journal of Speech, Language and the Law*, 4(2), 287–302.
Ehrlich, S., Eades, D., & Ainsworth, J. (2016). *Discursive constructions of consent in the legal process*. Oxford, UK: Oxford University Press.
Fisher, R. P., Geiselman, R. E., & Amador, M. (1989). Field test of the cognitive interview: Enhancing the recollections of actual victims and witnesses of crime. *Journal of Applied Psychology*, 74, 291–297.
Frankel, R. (1990). Talking in interviews: A dispreference for patient-initiated questions in physician-patient encounters. In G. Psathas (Ed.), *Interaction competence* (pp. 231–262). Washington, DC: University Press of America.

Geiselman, R. E., Fisher, R. P., MacKinnon, D. P., & Holland, H. L. (1986). Enhancement of eyewitness memory with the cognitive interview. *American Journal of Psychology, 99,* 385–401.

Gibbons, J. (1996). Distortions of the police interview process revealed by video-tape. *Forensic Linguistics: The International Journal of Speech, Language and the Law, 3*(2), 289–298.

Goffman, E. (1974). *Frame analysis.* New York: Harper and Row.

Goffman, E. (1981). *Forms of talk.* Philadelphia, PA: University of Pennsylvania Press.

Goodman-Delahunty, J., & Howes, L. M. (2014). Social persuasion to develop rapport in high-stakes interviews: Qualitative analyses of Asian-Pacific practices. *Policing and Society, 26*(3), 1–21. doi:10.1080/10439463.2014.942848

Grice, H. P. (1975). Logic and conversation. In P. Cole & J. L. Morgan (Eds.), *Speech acts (syntax and semantics volume III)* (pp. 41–58). New York: Academic Press.

Griffiths, A., & Milne, R. (2006). Will it all end in tiers? Police interviews with suspects in Britain. In T. Williamson (Ed.), *Investigative interviewing: Rights, research and regulation* (pp. 167–189). Cullompton, UK; Portland, OR: Willan.

Hager, E. (2017). A major player in law enforcement says it will stop using a method that's been linked to false confessions. *Business Insider.* Retrieved from https://www.business insider.com/reid-technique-false-confessions-law-enforcement-2017-3?IR=T

Hartwig, M., Granhag, P. A., & Luke, T. (2014). Strategic use of evidence during investigative interviews: The state of the science. In D. C. Raskin, C. R. Honts, & J. C. Kircher (Eds.), *Credibility assessment: Scientific research and applications* (pp. 1–36). San Diego, CA: Elsevier Academic Press.

Heydon, G. (1997). Participation frameworks, discourse features and embedded requests in police V.A.T.E. interviews with children. *Monash University Linguistics Papers, 1*(2), 21–31.

Heydon, G. (2002). The myth of the linguistic lie detector. *Monash University Linguistics Papers, 2*(2), 55–62.

Heydon, G. (2005a). Establishing the structure of police evidentiary interviews with suspects. *Forensic Linguistics: The International Journal of Speech, Language and the Law, 11*(1), 27–49.

Heydon, G. (2005b). *The language of police interviewing: A critical analysis.* New York: Palgrave Macmillan.

Heydon, G. (2012). Helping the police with their enquiries: Enhancing the investigative interview with linguistic research. *Police Journal: A Quarterly Review for the Police of the World, 85*(2), 101–122. doi:10.1350/pojo.2012.85.2.581

Hill, J. A., & Moston, S. (2011). Police perceptions of investigative interviewing: Training needs and operational practices in Australia. *The British Journal of Forensic Practice, 13*(2), 72–83.

Horvath, F., Blair, J., & Buckley, J. P. (2008). The behavioural analysis interview: Clarifying the practice, theory and understanding of its use and effectiveness. *International Journal of Police Science & Management, 10*(1), 101–118.

Inbau, F., Reid, J., Buckley, J., & Jayne, B. (2011). *Criminal interrogation and confessions.* Burlington, MA: Jones & Bartlett Publishers.

Jefferson, G. (1972). Side sequences. In D. N. Sudnow (Ed.), *Studies in social interaction* (pp. 294–338). New York, NY: Free Press.

Jefferson, G. (1984). On stepwise transition from talk about a trouble to inappropriately next-positioned matters. In J. M. Atkinson & J. Heritage (Eds.), *Structures of social action: Studies in conversation analysis* (pp. 191–222). Cambridge: Cambridge University Press.

Jefferson, G. (1988). On the sequential organization of troubles-talk in ordinary conversation. *Social Problems, 35*(4), 418–441.

Johnson, A. (2008). 'From where we're sat... ': Negotiating narrative transformation through interaction in police interviews with suspects. *Text & Talk, 28*(3), 327–349. doi:10.1515/Text.2008.016

Kaplan, J. P., Green, G. M., Cunningham, C. D., & Levi, J. N. (1995). Bringing linguistics into judicial decision-making: Semantic analysis submitted to the Supreme Court. *Forensic Linguistics: The International Journal of Speech, Language and the Law, 2*(1), 81–98.

Kebbell, M. (1997). Why do the police interview eyewitnesses? Interview objectives and the evaluation of eyewitness performance. *The Journal of Psychology, 131*(6), 595–601.

Levi, J. N. (1994). Language as evidence: The linguist as expert witness in North American courts. *Forensic Linguistics: The International Journal of Speech, Language and the Law, 1*(1), 1–26.

Levinson, S. C. (1988). Putting linguistics on a proper footing: Explorations in Goffman's concepts of participation. In P. Drew & A. Wootton (Eds.), *Erving Goffman: Exploring the interaction order* (pp. 161–227). Cambridge: Polity Press.

Mason, M. (2013). Can I get a lawyer? A suspect's use of indirect requests in a custodial setting. *International Journal of Speech, Language & the Law, 20*(2), 203–227. doi:10.1558/ijsll.v20i2.203

Meissner, C. A., & Kassin, S. M. (2004). "You're guilty, so just confess!" Cognitive and behavioural confirmation biases in the interrogation room. In G. D. Lassiter (Ed.), *Interrogations, confessions, and entrapment* (pp. 85–106). New York: Kluwer Academic.

Milne, R., & Bull, R. (1999). *Investigative interviewing: Psychology and practice*. Chichester; New York: Wiley.

Muniroh, R. D. D., & Aziz, E. A. (2016). The contemporary practices of Indonesian police interviewing of witnesses. In D. Walsh, G. E. Oxburgh, A. D. Redlich, & T. Myklebust (Eds.), *International developments and practices in investigative interviewing and interrogation volume 1: Victims and witnesses* (pp. 7–18). New York: Routledge.

Oxburgh, G. (2016). *Communication in investigative and legal contexts: Integrated approaches from forensic psychology, linguistics and law enforcement*. Chichester, West Sussex, UK: John Wiley & Sons.

Pearse, J., & Gudjonsson, G. H. (1996). Police interviewing techniques at two South London police stations. *Psychology, Crime & Law, 3*, 63–74.

Powell, M., & Thomson, D. M. (1994). Children's eyewitness-memory research: Implications for practice. *Families in Society: The Journal of Contemporary Human Services*, April, 204–215.

Ricciardi, L., & Demos, M. (2015). *Making a murderer*. Netflix and Synthesis Films.

Sacks, H. (1987). On the preferences for agreement and contiguity in sequences in conversation. In G. Button & J. Lee (Eds.), *Talk and social organisation* (pp. 54–69). Clevedon; Philadelphia, PA: Multilingual Matters Ltd.

Sacks, H. (1992). *Lectures on conversation*. Cambridge, MA: Blackwell Publishers.

Sacks, H., Schegloff, E., & Jefferson, G. (1974). A simplest systematics for the organisation of turn-taking for conversation. *Language, 50*(4), 696–735.

Schegloff, E. A. (1968). Sequencing in conversational openings1. *American Anthropologist, 70*(6), 1075–1095.

Schollum, M. (2005). *Investigative interviewing: The literature*. Wellington, New Zealand: Office of the Commissioner of Police.

Shepherd, E. (1993). Resistance in interviews: The contribution of police perceptions and behaviour. In P. Mathias (Ed.), *Aspects of police interviewing* (pp. 5–12). Leicester: The British Psychological Society.

Shuy, R. W. (1998). *The language of confession, interrogation, and deception*. Thousand Oaks, CA: Sage.

Shuy, R. W. (2017). *Deceptive ambiguity by police and prosecutors*. New York: Oxford University Press.

Snook, B., Eastwood, J., Stinson, M., Tedeschini, J., & House, J. C. (2010). Reforming investigative interviewing in Canada. *Canadian Journal of Criminology and Criminal Justice, 52*(2), 215–229.

Snook, B., House, J. C., MacDonald, S., & Eastwood, J. (2012). Police witness interview training, supervision, and feedback: A survey of Canadian police officers. *Canadian Journal of Criminology and Criminal Justice, 54*(3), 363–372. doi:10.3138/cjccj.2011.E.13

Snook, B., & Keating, K. (2011). A field study of adult witness interviewing practices in a Canadian police organization. *Legal and Criminological Psychology, 16*(1), 160–172. doi:10.1348/135532510x497258

Snook, B., Luther, K., Quinlan, H., & Milne, R. (2012). LET 'EM TALK! A field study of police questioning practices of suspects and accused persons. *Criminal Justice and Behavior, 39*(10), 1328–1339. doi:10.1177/0093854812449216

Solan, L., M. (1998). Linguistic experts as semantic tour guides. *Forensic Linguistics: The International Journal of Speech, Language and the Law, 5*(2), 87–106.

Stephenson, G. M., & Moston, S. J. (1993). Attitudes and assumptions of police officers when questioning criminal subjects. In P. Mathias (Ed.), *Aspects of police interviewing* (pp. 30–36). Leicester: The British Psychological Society.

Vrij, A., Granhag, P. A., Mann, S., & Leal, S. (2011). Outsmarting the liars: Toward a cognitive lie detection approach. *Current Directions in Psychological Science, 20*(1), 28–32. doi:10.1177/0963721410391245

Vrij, A., Hope, L., & Fisher, R. P. (2014). Eliciting reliable information in investigative interviews. *Policy Insights from the Behavioral and Brain Sciences, 1*(1), 129–136.

Vrij, A., Mann, S., & Fisher, R. P. (2006). An empirical test of the behaviour analysis interview. *Law and Human Behavior, 30*(3), 329–345.

Westera, N. J., Kebbell, M. R., & Milne, B. (2011). Interviewing witnesses: Do investigative and evidential requirements concur? *The British Journal of Forensic Practice, 13*(2), 103–113.

Williams, J. W. (2000). Interrogating justice: A critical analysis of the police interrogation and its role in the criminal justice process. *Canadian Journal of Criminology-Revue Canadienne De Criminologie, 42*(2), 209–240.

Woolls, D., & Coulthard, M. (1998). Tools for the trade. *Forensic Linguistics: The International Journal of Speech, Language and the Law, 5*(1), 33–57.

Wright, R., & Powell, M. B. (2007). What makes a good investigative interviewer of children? A comparison of police officers' and experts' perceptions. *Policing: An International Journal of Police Strategies & Management, 30*(1), 21–31.

Yuan, C. (2010). Avoiding revictimization: Shifting from police interrogations to police interviewing in China. *International Journal of Speech Language and the Law, 16*(2), 297. doi:10.1558/ijsll.v16i2.293

4 Lie detection and linguistics

Introduction

In Chapter 3 we examined different approaches to police interviewing training that have been taken by police academies on either side of the Atlantic. A discourse analytic approach was useful in identifying the dominant features of the PEACE and Reid methods of interviewing training used in the United Kingdom and the United States, respectively. An important difference between these two methods was the reliance in the Reid method on the behavioural analysis interview (BAI), which seeks to separate liars from truth-tellers prior to applying more coercive interrogation techniques to those subjects who are believed to be concealing information from police. Prior research has described the importance of lie detection to the Reid method of interviewing and demonstrated that this leaves police officers vulnerable to the allure of 'quick fix' lie detection courses (Snook, Eastwood, Stinson, Tedeschini, & House, 2010). Many such courses are available to law enforcement officers especially in North America, and systematic studies of the various techniques that are taught have consistently shown that they are ineffective at separating liars from truth-tellers (Porter & Yuille, 1996; Vrij, Granhag, Mann, & Leal, 2011b). This results in a situation where the dominant form of interviewing training in the United States – the Reid method – requires a specialisation that is demonstrably unattainable: the human lie detector. In the United Kingdom, interviewing training has resolved this conflict by removing the need for lie detection from the interviewing training. Professor John Baldwin's landmark review and report on police interviewing and interrogation practices in the United Kingdom in the early 1990s addressed the problem of the human lie detector when he recommended a definitive shift away from 'sophisticated approaches to questioning' based on popular psychology and unproven lie detection techniques that are 'worthless – even dangerous' (Baldwin, 1993, p. 350). Not surprisingly, the advent of the PEACE model that followed paid no heed to assessments of 'body language' or 'non-verbal indicators of deception' in the police interview dynamic (Baldwin, 1993, p. 350). Instead, and thanks to pioneers such as the late Tom Williamson, the police investigator as human lie detector was forced to step aside and make way for the detective as information gatherer (Williamson, 2006).

The role of forensic linguistics in this landscape became more relevant when the means of lie detection began to include linguistic indicators of deception. There are several such methods that rely on the analysis of a written statement from the subject and apply criteria to the text in order to separate statements based on actual events from statements based on the author's imagination. The methods are based on the Undeutsch hypothesis which states that 'the memory of a real-life self-experienced event differs in content and quality from a fabricated or imagined event' (Amado, Arce, & Fariña, 2015; Undeutsch, 1989). Criteria-based Content Analysis (CBCA) is one such method (Amado et al., 2015; Steller, 1989). Another method that is popular with police forces is Scientific Content Analysis (SCAN) developed by an ex-Israeli Defence Force officer, Avinoam Sapir (Sapir, 1987). Repeated laboratory and field studies have attempted to test the reliability of these methods (Porter & Yuille, 1996; Vrij, 2008) with perhaps the most comprehensive study of SCAN conducted by the UK Home Office (Smith, 2001). While Porter and Yuille (1996) tested whether the criteria used in the SCAN method (as well as CBCA and Statement Validity Analysis) were able to differentiate deceptive texts from truthful texts, the Home Office study (Smith, 2001) tested the abilities of trained SCAN users against untrained detectives. Although Armistead (2011) finds that there are weaknesses in the presentation of Smith's statistics, both he and Smith find that the SCAN method is of questionable efficacy. Smith found that trained SCAN users did not perform better than experienced detectives with no SCAN training. Armistead disputed the statistical significance reported by Smith, but conceded that there remained no study that had confirmed the validity of the method.

In addition to methods that attempt to detect deception in written documents, there are methods of lie detection that purport to detect deception in spoken language using linguistic indicators such as pitch, equivocal language and latency response (Ekman, Friesen, & Scherer, 1976). These too have been subjected to laboratory and other testing, mainly by psychologists (Scherer, Feldstein, Bond, & Rosenthal, 1985), but are relevant to linguists interested in studying deception (see for instance Reynolds & Rendle-Short, 2011).

Approach to the problem

If we define the problem as 'Does SCAN work?,' or 'Can we accurately detect deception using linguistic cues?' then there is an opportunity for forensic linguistic researchers to conduct a comprehensive set of laboratory and field tests of the SCAN method or other methods that rely on language cues to detect deception. Such research would require laboratory testing using an experimental model to generate statements with variable truth conditions and known ground truths. There are many such studies described in the deception literature that have been developed, mainly by psychologists (Hartwig et al., 2011; Leal, Vrij, Mann, & Fisher, 2011; Smith, 2001; Vrij, Evans, Akehurst, & Mann, 2004; Vrij, Granhag, Mann, & Leal, 2011a). However, a common criticism of these studies is that they fail to replicate the real-world conditions of a police investigation – they lack ecological validity – and in particular, that the stakes are never high enough for the subjects to display genuine physiological, psychological or linguistic signs of deception (or truthfulness) in their responses (Horvath, Blair, & Buckley, 2008). For this reason, field studies are also necessary, though notoriously difficult to conduct. Some studies of deception have relied on footage of appeals for help during missing-person investigations (Wright Whelan, Wagstaff, & Wheatcroft, 2014). In these broadcasts, relatives of the victim make an appeal to the public, often describing the events leading to the person's disappearance. In some cases, the person speaking in the video is later proven to have been responsible for the victim's disappearance or death. In many other cases, the speaker is definitively ruled out as the offender. These broadcast appeals thus become a publicly available data source including samples of speech from both truth-tellers and liars where ground truth data are available and the stakes are very high. This is not a useful data source for an examination of SCAN, since SCAN operates on written texts produced by the subject in relation to the events in question. But for those interested in studying linguistic indicators of deception in speech, the data provide an opportunity for ecological validity in the design.

However, studies that test the efficacy of a method or linguistic cue to deceit are not the only approach to the problem. Forensic linguistic research can also contribute to the theoretical understanding of deceptive language.

One of the notable features of deception research involving linguistic indicators is that it tends to be conducted by psychologists rather than linguists (Vrij, 2008). Very often, analyses of verbal indicators of deception form part of a broader study of deceptive behaviour and the explanations for the use of linguistic cues indicating deception or truthfulness are explained in relation to theories of cognition or behaviour. For instance, speech errors, which some researchers have found to be positively correlated with deception, are explained in relation to cognitive load (Vrij et al., 2011b; Vrij et al., 2008). This seems consistent with psycholinguistic research identifying speech errors that occur mid-utterance as indicators that the speaker is increasing their cognitive load as they formulate their next utterance (Postma, 2000).[1] However, some of the psychological explanations for linguistic cues to deception seem less convincing. For instance, DePaulo et al. (2003) associate equivocal language (language that conveys vagueness or uncertainty such as *perhaps*, *maybe*, *sort of*) with the act of 'distancing' the speaker from the subject of their speech. This is the same theoretical basis for many of the criteria used to identify deceptive language in the SCAN method such as the writer avoiding the use of the first person, or switching from the first person singular *I* to the first person plural *we*. Another example, drawn from the sample analysis provided on the SCAN website, involves the deceptive writer using the pronoun *it* to describe an object, rather than a specific noun phrase (Laboratory for Scientific Interrogation Inc., n.d.-c). However from a linguistic perspective, these analyses seem problematic. For instance, the set of lexemes that convey vagueness or uncertainty can function pragmatically to indicate politeness, not just 'distance from the subject.'

Sociolinguists have long understood the relationship between grammatical indirectness and politeness (Brown & Levinson, 1987). How might a practitioner in the field, such as a police investigator interviewing a suspect, differentiate between markers of indirect speech that are intended to indicate politeness and markers of indirect speech that indicate the suspect's desire to distance themselves from the topic of the utterance? Returning to the SCAN method, it hardly takes a linguist to see that a writer will avoid repeating the complete noun phrase for an object and instead will usually substitute a pronoun such as *it*. The example given on the SCAN website reads as follows:

> **Excerpt 4.1 From www.lsiscan.com 'Can you find the confession in this statement?'**
>
> My car was parked out the front of the house with the alarm set. I last saw it around 8 PM Sunday. I woke up in the morning and discovered it missing around 9 AM.

The proposed 'solution' to this case focuses on the rendition of the noun phrase *my car* as *it* in the second and third sentences. The accompanying text states that '[t]o use the neutral pronoun "it" might indicate that the last time the subject saw the car it did not have driving ability' (Laboratory for Scientific Interrogation Inc., n.d.-b). The irony of the solution containing the very same rendition of the NP *the car* as a pronoun *it* ('...the last time the subject saw the car **it** did not...') is apparently lost on the website's authors.

A linguist can name the phenomenon – anaphora – but almost any educated writer of English or student of English literature will be able to identify this as a normal use of language and not a cue to deception. Unsurprisingly, Porter and Yuille's (1996) above-mentioned tests of the SCAN criteria did not find any of these cues to be positively correlated with deception. In short, by looking at the grammatical and pragmatic, rather than the behavioural, basis for these linguistic cues, we can see that either there is little theoretical support for their reliability as indicators of deceit, or that they are unlikely to be of much practical use in the field because they do not form a distinct linguistic set of lexemes.

These observations do not diminish the value of research that tests the SCAN criteria or investigates the linguistic theory (or lack thereof) supporting SCAN and other methods that use linguistic cues to deception. However, as the many studies cited in this chapter indicate, there is a substantial and authoritative corpus of research literature dating back several decades that challenges the validity of lie detection, linguistic or otherwise, and it seems to have had a depressingly small impact on the use of such methods in law enforcement and the justice system more broadly. Polygraph tests are still used around the world despite being condemned as unreliable in studies dating back almost to its invention (National Research Council, 2003), so it seems optimistic to hope that further scientific publications

64 Police procedures

on deceptive language will do anything to curb the use of unreliable methods in the field. Indeed, as far back as 1998, Roger Shuy demonstrated that the SCAN methodology is fundamentally flawed and inconsistent with sociolinguistic theory (Shuy, 1998). In particular, Shuy (1998) finds that the methodology fails to take into account sociocultural variation in language use and ascribes meanings to language features that are unsupported by sociolinguistic research and which grossly generalise the functions of certain utterances or speech patterns by individuals. Shuy's findings are further supported by Vrij, whose work evaluates the effectiveness of SCAN as a training technique (2008, pp. 289–291). Despite these critical appraisals of SCAN, it continues to be a popular training course for law enforcement officers across the United States, as a glance at the website shows (Figure 4.1).

	LSI Basic Course on SCAN	LSI SCAN Advanced Workshop
Austin, TX	July 16-18, 2018	July 18-19, 2018
Springfield, MO	July 23-25, 2018	July 25-26, 2018
Columbus, OH area	Aug 6-8, 2018	Aug 8-9, 2018
Philadelphia, PA area	Aug 13-15, 2018	Aug 15-16, 2018
Salt Lake City, UT area	Aug 27-29, 2018	Aug 29-30, 2018
Washington, DC area	Oct 15-17, 2018	Oct 17-18, 2018
Detroit, MI area	Oct 22-24, 2018	Oct 24-25, 2018
Raleigh, NC*	Oct 29-31, 2018	Oct 31 - Nov 1, 2018
Tallahassee, FL*	Nov 5-7, 2018	Nov 7-8, 2018
Oklahoma City, OK*	Nov 13-15, 2018	Nov 15-16, 2018
Houston, TX*	Nov 26-28, 2018	Nov 28-29, 2018
San Antonio, TX*	Dec 3-5, 2018	Dec 5-6, 2018
Miami, FL*	Dec 10-12, 2018	Dec 12-13, 2018
Albuquerque, NM*	Dec 10-12, 2018	Dec 12-13, 2018
Phoenix, AZ area*	Feb 11-13, 2019	Feb 13-14, 2019
Fort Worth, TX	Mar 4-6, 2019	Mar 6-7, 2019
New Orleans, LA area*	Mar 11-13, 2019	Mar 13-14, 2019
Detroit, MI area*	Mar 18-20, 2019	Mar 20-21, 2019
Morristown, NJ area*	Mar 25-27, 2019	Mar 27-28, 2019
Washington, DC area*	Apr 1-3, 2019	Apr 3-4, 2019
Lansing, MI	May 6-8, 2019	May 8-9, 2019
Toronto, ON area*	May 13-15, 2019	May 15-16, 2019
Calgary, AB*	May 27-29, 2019	May 29-30, 2019
Seattle, WA*	June 17-19, 2019	June 19-20, 2019
Boise, ID*	June 24-26, 2019	June 26-27, 2019
Los Angeles, CA*	July 8-10, 2019	July 10-11, 2019
Austin, TX area*	July 16-18, 2019	July 18-19, 2019

Figure 4.1 SCAN courses in the United States 2018–2019 from http://www.lsiscan.com/id25_the_lsi_basic_course_on_scan.htm accessed 4 October 2018.

Instead of further critical analysis of the SCAN method, therefore, we might approach the problem from a different linguistic perspective and undertake a critical discourse analysis (CDA) of the language used to promote lie detection, and in particular the mythologising of the 'human lie detector.' Perhaps justice departments would be better equipped to understand and address the scientific flaws in their lie detection toolkit if they could see the underlying assumptions that support the lie detection industry to promote faulty tools to law enforcement officers. In a CDA framework, the importance of examining discourses for underlying assumptions that might constitute mythologies has been well established (Fairclough & Wodak, 1997; van Dijk, 1996; Wodak, 1996b). Different sub-types of 'institutional discourse' are found to exhibit evidence of mythologies being created and maintained by participants in the discourse.

Baldwin, in his discussion of a criminological examination of 600 police interviews in Britain, finds that the existence of a mythology surrounding police training in the area of interviewing suspects is supported by the fact that 'debates on the crucial question of interview procedures...have tended to be dominated by views from the police service. However, many of these views have proved on analysis, to be misconceived or erroneous' (1993, p. 334). In further support of these claims, Bull (1989) discusses several studies which find that training in detecting deception has no significant effect on police officers' performance, despite the claims of texts aimed at police officers and recruits. In reference to two unpublished studies which suggest that experience (as opposed to training) can make a difference in performance, Bull notes that '[u]ntil a number of publications in refereed journals appear demonstrating that training enhances the detection of deception, it seems that some police recruitment advertisements and police training books are deceiving their readers' (1989, p. 97). As established in the literature cited previously, such publications have not been forthcoming in the three decades since Bull made this assertion.

As Wodak (1996a) points out, the danger of a mythology of discursive practice in an institutional setting is that it can actually prevent the organisation from meeting its goals – beliefs about the discursive practices in an organisation can be counterproductive when they are erroneous because they create behaviour in participants which may be inappropriate to the real-life situation.

While the problems associated with using questionable techniques of analysis to ascertain the truth of an interviewee's statement may be rather obvious, other practices are equally deserving of scrutiny perhaps the more so because their effects are deeper and often hidden from the casual observer. For instance, the very belief that it is possible to detect truth accurately is itself dangerous, as it encourages police institutions to continue to search for 'reliable' methods of lie detection, when none exist. In a further example of assumptions underlying the discourse of police interviewing, Bull (1989) cites several contemporary newspapers and published articles which strongly suggest that the detection of deception is straightforward and simple – a claim which Bull rejects.

Identifying research questions

Taking a CDA approach to this problem means that our research questions seek to explore the links between the language used to promote lie detection courses and the assumptions that underlie police institutional discourse, particularly in relation to interviewing and establishing credibility. Thus our key research questions might be:

1 What are the assumptions that underlie police institutional discourse in relation to detecting deceit?
2 Are these assumptions present in the promotional material for a prominent lie detection course (SCAN) and if so, how do they manifest in the discourse?
3 What are the implications for policymakers seeking to minimise the use of unscientific methods of police interviewing?

Data collection

Our data for this type of study are predominantly publicly available advertising or course materials and police institutional policy documents. In the example given here, we will analyse advertising material that is publicly available from The Laboratory for Scientific Interrogation, Inc. (LSI), the organisation that developed the SCAN course (Sapir, 1987). The LSI website (www.lsiscan.com) advertises courses in Sapir's SCAN technique that are regularly delivered in the United States, as indicated previously, but can also be delivered at centres in England, Belgium, Israel, Mexico and Australia (Laboratory for Scientific Interrogation Inc., n.d.-a). The focus of this paper will be a close examination of the SCAN information page (Laboratory for Scientific Interrogation Inc., n.d.-c). This page of the LSI SCAN site constitutes the first point of contact that interested members of the public are likely to have with SCAN once they have opened the home page, and the text contained therein functions to introduce and make claims about the use of SCAN. Except where otherwise indicated, all subsequent references to the SCAN online materials are referring to this page.

For the analysis of the final research question, we will draw on policy documents that indicate the different ways in which the two primary interviewing methods used in the United States and England, respectively, have each addressed the underlying assumptions that support the myth of the human lie detector.

Data analysis

Our first research question asks: *what are the assumptions that underlie police institutional discourse in relation to detecting deceit?* Prior research indicates that there is a set of assumptions about deception that underlies the interview-related beliefs of people both inside and outside of justice institutions. These beliefs about deceptive behaviour and lie detection are pervasive in popular culture and the media, as evidenced by the many instances of stories involving lie detection methods being reported in the press as though such methods are scientifically valid (for a recent example see Morris, 2018). Researchers in this area (Auburn, Drake, & Willig, 1995; Baldwin, 1993; Bull, 1989; Bull & Milne, 2004; Shuy, 1998) have suggested that there are several such assumptions underlying police interviewing techniques. These assumptions can be summarised as follows:

1   that it is possible to detect when someone is being deceptive by examining their use of language;
2   that to detect when someone is being deceptive is simple;
3   that it is possible to be trained to detect deception in a person's language use;
4   that it is possible to apply successfully a binary test to human behaviour which works as well as, for instance, a physical or chemical test;
5   that deception is a binary behaviour;
6   that there is one objective version of events adequately represented by the police version or statement of evidence, and;
7   that the suspect is guilty and behaving deceptively to cover up their involvement in the crime.

Insofar as marketing a training course which teaches 'lie detection' is concerned, assumption 3, *that it is possible to be trained to detect deception in a person's language use*, is the most critical to support and the remaining assumptions provide a network of support for this one. For instance, in order to learn a technique, it is first necessary that the technique is possible and exists, and this is the purpose of assumption 1. A training course will be made simpler and more attractive to potential clients if the technique is simple (assumption 2). Assumptions 4, 5 and 6 all concern the casting of deceit and truth as binary by nature, and this is used in the marketing of the method as 'scientific' (see below). The final assumption, assumption 7, addresses a slightly different set of issues as it relates to the interviewer's conduct within the framework of the interview, rather than to aspects of training surrounding the interview procedure. Nonetheless it is appropriate that this assumption be considered as part of our investigation as it is still part of the mythology attached to the marketing of SCAN rather than being part of its methodology.

Our second research question requires us to take a discourse analytic approach to the SCAN promotional material to identify evidence that any of the assumptions identified above are underlying the messages on the website. In this analysis, each of the assumptions is dealt with, in turn, below.

a. Detecting deception is possible

As the whole marketing scheme is based on the premise that it is possible to detect deception in a person's (written) statement, this assumption can be said to underlie the actual existence of the LSI website. Therefore it is perhaps more interesting to examine some of the other assumptions said to contribute to the mythology of police interviewing.

b. Detecting deception is simple

The opening sentence, beneath the heading, adequately demonstrates the presence of the assumption that detecting deception is simple: 'SCAN (Scientific Content Analysis) will solve every case for you quickly and easily.' This assumption underlies the description of the technique as a three step process, and the way in which the most complex part of the technique – the analysis – is treated as half of one step: '3. **Analyze the statement** and solve the case.' (emphasis added)

The assumption that deception detection is simple is strongly supported by the metaphor of SCAN as a visual technique. For instance, there are two acronyms used for the products, SCAN and VIEW (Verbal Inquiry – the Effective Witness). Both seem highly contrived, as acronyms often are, and can therefore be discussed as labels chosen for their connotational qualities by the Laboratory for Scientific Investigation. The use of the name SCAN implies an analysis comprising a short, visual examination of the text, while VIEW does not imply any cognitive digestion of the text at all, merely that it is seen. Both support the assumption that detecting deception is a simple procedure requiring minimal analytic work on behalf of the investigator. Furthermore, *scan* has the technological meaning of a computer-assisted process, adding a sense of automation to the description of the methodology.

This latter aspect of the 'simplicity' assumption is extended by the use of phrases which suggest that SCAN itself is an animated entity which undertakes work on behalf of the investigator: 'SCAN GETS THE TRUTH...SCAN is the tool that will give you...SCAN will show you.' This is even expanded to include the animation of the answer which will literally 'jump out at you' and '[e]very word in the subject's statement [which] will "talk" to you and show you the answer.'

The assumption of a simple process is further underlined by the continuation of the 'visual technique' metaphor in the use of phrases such as 'SCAN will show you.'

c. One truth

As the browser opens the LSI SCAN webpage, the text immediately presents perhaps the most powerful argument in favour of the SCAN method – that there is one objective and true version of an interviewee's statement which correlates exactly to events that have occurred in the real world, labelled THE TRUTH.

This assumption (6) is reiterated throughout the page, generally through the use of the phrase the truth, but also in the more suggestive phrase the answer, which implies a question-answer sequence in the process when none is used.

This assumption includes a concept of 'truth' in an interviewee's statement being a binary quality which, together with the assumption that deception is binary behaviour, can be seen to support the fourth assumption that it is possible to apply a 'scientific' test for the presence or absence of truth.

Lie detection and linguistics 69

Auburn et al.'s (1995) research on a 'preferred version' of the suspect's narrative is also related to the assumption of 'one truth.' That one version can be said to be preferred assumes that one objectively true version of the events exists, or can be said to exist. That is, in order to select a preferred version, the police must begin the process by making an assumption that there is such a version that corresponds to a true and objective view of the events.

d. Detecting deception can be done 'scientifically'

This assumption is most clearly stated under the second heading: 'How is scan different from other techniques?' Here the claim is made quite boldly that SCAN is scientific – a consistent formula which gives consistent results. Interestingly, the possibility that something can be scientific and complicated, or scientific and inexact, is not explored.

e. Deception is binary behaviour

Many sections of the text seem to reflect this assumption. SCAN is described as a tool that will show you: 'whether the subject is truthful or deceptive' and 'whether or not the subject was involved in the crime.' This includes, perhaps more worryingly, an assumption that if an interviewee is said to be untruthful in part of their statement, then they must always be being untruthful. It does not allow for partial truths, or statements that may be based on a false premise, for instance.

This assumption of deception being binary behaviour is tied to an assumption that all interviewees will produce an undistorted statement. This is a more complex assumption because it is in fact contradictory. On the one hand, readers are asked to believe that whether or not the interviewee is lying about the 'facts' of the incident, no other aspect of the statement will be distorted. For instance, there is no mention of the possibility that, in order to deceive the interviewer into believing a false statement, the interviewee might deliberately use the speech patterns that are said to indicate truthfulness. Therein lies the paradox: on the one hand, the method assumes that the deceitful interviewee will be willing and able to lie about the events in question, but on the other hand there is an assumption that such an interviewee will be completely oblivious to the possibility that effective lying would include the use of particular speech patterns.

f. The guilty subject

Perhaps the most endemic assumption and most widely recognised aspect of the mythology of police interviewing (Auburn et al., 1995; Baldwin, 1993; Settle, 1990; Shuy, 1998) is that the subject is guilty and s/he is lying to conceal her/his guilt. This assumption is at work in the SCAN page in phrases such as 'SCAN will show you:….what information the subject is concealing.' Several references to 'solving the case' using SCAN assume that the subject making the statement is one whose involvement is critical to the case. In most investigations, the person whose statement can most successfully 'solve' the case is the guilty party.

The third research question asks: *what are the implications for policy-makers seeking to minimise the use of unscientific methods of police interviewing?* Pressure is exerted on members of the police force to maintain order in our society – that is their job. Yet the same society must place heavy restrictions on the manner in which order might be maintained or risk degrading the quality of life of its citizens (Settle, 1990). This conflict between the duty of the police officer to maintain order and the necessity to do so within a restrictive framework of laws occasionally produces questionable procedures such as those highlighted by other research into police interviewing (Cooke, 1996; Eades, 1994; Gibbons, 1996; Meissner & Kassin, 2004). Where these procedures have been analysed and a clear abuse of power has been identified, then steps may be taken to redress the balance. For example, the distortion of evidence discussed in Linell & Jonsson's (1991) study (which is similar to distortions found in many other case studies cited) might be avoided by using the original audio recording of the interview as evidence, rather than a written statement based on a transcription of the recording.

However, the use of SCAN or other 'linguistic lie detectors' in police interviewing presents more subtle problems for reformists. In this case, the conflict between Law and Order leads to a much more complex abuse of power towards organisational ends which occurs at a policy, rather than at an individual level. Whereas an individual officer may come under scrutiny for engaging in the sort of questionable behaviour described by the researchers mentioned above, it is the nature of mythologies about institutional practices that they influence behaviour at an institutional level, often at a policy level. Thus, in the case of SCAN, it is the police force as an institution whose actions require scrutiny. In order to demonstrate that an abuse of power has even taken place, it must first be shown not just that SCAN and its ilk are methodologically flawed, but that the decision to implement training in the use of a 'human lie detector' is itself based on false assumptions about language behaviour.

If we examine the two most common interviewing training regimes, PEACE and the Reid method (see Chapter 3), we can describe how each of these approaches addresses the underlying assumptions identified above. In the first case, the PEACE and the cognitive interviewing approach, the UK Home Office publish materials governing police practices developed and distributed through the Association of Chief Police Officers (ACPO). ACPO effectively has oversight of interviewing training across all police stations in England and Wales, where the PEACE model was developed. As discussed in Chapter 3, there are publically available copies of the ACPO Principles of Investigative Interviewing that guide all such training and practice. The College of Policing (College of Policing UK, 2018) identifies the Principles of Investigative Interviewing, which were revised in 2007, as follows:

Lie detection and linguistics 71

> i The aim of investigative interviewing is to obtain accurate and reliable accounts from victims, witnesses or suspects about matters under police investigation.
> ii Investigators must act fairly when questioning victims, witnesses or suspects. Vulnerable people must be treated with particular consideration at all times.
> iii Investigative interviewing should be approached with an investigative mindset. Accounts obtained from the person who is being interviewed should always be tested against what the interviewer already knows or what can reasonably be established.
> iv When conducting an interview, investigators are free to ask a wide range of questions in order to obtain material which may assist an investigation.
> v Investigators should recognise the positive impact of an early admission in the context of the criminal justice system.
> vi Investigators are not bound to accept the first answer given. Questioning is not unfair merely because it is persistent.
> vii Even when the right of silence is exercised by a suspect, investigators have a responsibility to put questions to them.
> (Published by the ACPO, Home Office, United Kingdom)

Immediately, it is clear that there is no mention of a 'search for truth' or even the notion of 'credibility.' The first principle describes the aim of a police interview as obtaining 'accurate and reliable accounts' from relevant people, and the third principle reiterates the need for reliability, as established through evidence external to the interview. There is an emphasis on the needs of the interviewee (Principle ii) and the need for unbiased and open-minded questioning (Principle iii) but otherwise the Principles are concerned with establishing what is reasonable behaviour for an interviewer in pursuit of 'accurate and reliable accounts.' There is reference to a 'wide range of questions,' to persistent questioning (so long as it is not otherwise unfair) and to encouraging an early admission. Notably perhaps, there is no use of the terms 'guilty,' 'innocent,' 'deception,' 'credibility,' 'confession' or 'conviction.' The Principles use language that emphasises the role of the investigator as an unbiased instrument of the justice system, and not an evaluator of truth or innocence in their own right.

While there is no equivalent document in the United States to the ACPO Principles of Investigative Interviewing, the textbooks and articles published by the Reid training organisation and additional authoritative texts such as the Training Key series published by the US-based International Association of Chiefs of Police can provide relevant material for this discussion. Chapter 3 of this volume presents a discussion of the Reid technique and the BAI, drawing on an article (Horvath et al., 2008) published with the purpose of illustrating how the BAI is intended to function. As discussed in Chapter 3, the authors of this article make it very clear that a central purpose of the Reid method (and police interviewing in general, in their view) is to assist investigators to identify truth and assess the credibility of interviewees. The article states, within the first few paragraphs, that '[w]hat and whom the police find credible are, at the core, the essence of the questions addressed in the police investigative task' (p. 101) and cite a range of sources to support this assertion (Ericson, 1981; Horvath & Meesig, 1996; Innes, 2003; Simon, 1991, all cited in Horvath et al., 2008: 101). The analysis of the BAI presented in Chapter 3 shows that the questions suggested for use in the interview are all intended to strategically separate truth-tellers from liars and indeed the article by Horvath et al. (2008) states that '[t]he purpose of the BAI is to help investigators sort those who are likely to be guilty from those who are not and thus to interrogate only those in the former category' (p. 102). To the extent that the Reid method can be regarded as a foundation of police interviewing in the United States (cf. Cleary & Warner, 2016), this document and the wider selection of training materials produced by the Reid organisation suggest that by comparison with the PEACE training method, the BAI is positioned consistently as a search for truth, with the credibility of the interviewee a key concern for the investigator. Other widely circulated training documents produced in the United States further support this position. The Training Key series mentioned above includes a publication on 'Assessing Witness Credibility' which prefaces the main text by stating that '[i]t is the investigator's responsibility to properly analyze a witness's credibility in order to complete a thorough investigation.' (International Association of Chiefs of Police, 2018).

Interpreting data

Our analysis of the institutional documents suggests that the approach to interviewing training by authorities in the United Kingdom is markedly different to the approach taken in the United States especially with regard to the issue of 'truth.' The Principles of Investigative Interviewing produced by the UK Home Office contain no mention of truth, but rather characterise the main function of the investigative interview as obtaining 'accurate and reliable accounts.' While it might be argued that 'accurate' is functionally equivalent to 'truthful,' the difference between these principles and the guidelines for police interviewing in the United States (Horvath et al., 2008; International Association of Chiefs of Police, 2018) is in the language describing interviewing behaviour. The Home Office document is careful not to suggest that the investigator has the responsibility for determining the honesty or inherent credibility of the interviewee. The account given by an interviewee 'should always be tested against' other evidence, but the investigator is not expected or encouraged to take up the role of 'human lie detector.' By contrast, 'the BAI is used to detect "liars"' (Horvath et al., 2008, p. 103). This discrepancy in the goals of the two types of interviewing leads to a difference in the type of supporting research or additional training that supports these methods. Police officers in England and Wales are provided with training based on cognitive psychology that provides a basic introduction to memory, cognition and language science and teaches them to use memory-enhancing techniques to elicit detailed narratives. Techniques such as the Strategic Use of Evidence (Hartwig, Granhag, & Luke, 2014) are suggested as appropriate methods to enhance opportunities to uncover discrepancies between an interviewee's account and other evidence, but 'lie detection' per se is not discussed as either possible or appropriate for police investigators.

The Reid method uses a highly accusatory interrogation technique to elicit a confession from a suspect, and therefore requires investigators to determine accurately which of their witnesses might be guilty so that only they, and not innocent people, will be subjected to the interrogation's nine steps. Hence, the police interview training industry, dominated by John E. Reid and Associates, has developed and promoted the BAI, which is used as a tool to separate the guilty from the innocent prior to the interrogation. Given that the science has consistently demonstrated the difficulty of this task, it is not surprising that a wide variety of lie detection courses are available to police officers in the United States and in other countries where officers are encouraged to believe that a core skill they must acquire is to become a 'human lie detector.'

Applications to legal practice and procedures

In the context of the Reid method of interviewing, the SCAN technique can be seen as providing investigators with a solution to an intractable problem: accurately and consistently separating truth-tellers from liars in order that only the guilty are pressured into confessing, and only the innocent are set free. In a system that assumes it is possible to detect deception, and accepts all the other assumptions that follow, as set out above, it becomes acceptable to use coercive questioning techniques, because only the guilty will be interrogated. The same reasoning is used to justify torture, and the Executive Order that in 2009 eliminated torture during the interrogation of detainees in the United States (Crook, 2009) seems at the time of writing to be under threat. In his 2016 presidential campaign, then-candidate Trump pledged to 'load [CIA Guantanamo Prison] up with some bad dudes' implying that all terror suspects are presumed guilty, and that he 'would bring back waterboarding, and I'd bring back a hell of a lot worse than waterboarding' (Garofoli, 2018). Here again, we see the reasoning that, if it is possible to detect deceit, then investigators can identify guilty parties and subject them to any level of coercive interrogation to obtain a confession.

The assumptions identified above relating to lie detection underlie a system of justice that can accept the elicitation of a confession using coercion and even physical torture by investigators because innocent people are presumed to be safe from this treatment. As to whether any human, guilty or not, is deserving of such treatment raises other equally important ethical questions, but the reliance on unproven lie detection methods in the justice system is made all the more dangerous – yet all the more likely – when the stakes are so high. The alternative, offered by the PEACE model, is an approach that prioritises the elicitation of a detailed account over the assessment of credibility. Using techniques and knowledge

74 *Police procedures*

based on scientific research findings, investigators can apply themselves to the task of assembling evidence that will be tested in the courts, rather than feeling under pressure to achieve the impossible and become a 'human lie detector.'

Final word

In the course of my career I have had the privilege of working with many dedicated and talented police officers. Without their insights, my work on police interviewing and other law enforcement processes would lack authenticity and real-world application. I therefore leave the final word on lie detection to one such officer, Det. John Tedeschini, whose pursuit of an evidence-based method of interviewing led him to question the reliability of everything he'd been taught about deception.

> 'Independent verification of a detail offered by a subject is the only foolproof deception detection method – this is why the best strategy for detecting deception is to elicit as full an account as possible' (Brandon, Wells, & Seale, 2018).
>
> As a novice investigator in the 1990s, the promise of virtually instant lie detection abilities was simply too good to pass up. Whether attending commercial training courses or sending away for training materials, the opportunity to become a 'human lie detector' was precisely the sort of edge I was looking for. After all, what's not to like about using the latest lie detection product to 'solve every case quickly and easily'?
>
> Decades later, it's painfully obvious that the edge I was searching for was right in front of me from the outset. Instead of the empty promises of exceptional lie detection abilities, the 'edge' was – and remains – a commitment to investigative interviewing fundamentals. Sound planning and preparation, rapport building, listening and productive questioning all serve as the foundation for an effective investigative interview.
>
> Importantly, adherence to core interviewing skills helps insulate interviewers from the fallacy of the 'human lie detector' while simultaneously placing them in a much stronger position to distinguish truth from lies. Although much progress has been made towards evidence-based training programs, practitioners should remain vigilant about what is being pitched their way. If it's too good to be true it usually is.
>
> John Tedeschini
Edmonton Police Service (retired)
Alberta, Canada

Note

1 Although note that Wright Whelan's study of high stakes lies found that the relationship between speech errors and deceptive statements was not statistically significant.

References

Amado, B. G., Arce, R., & Fariña, F. (2015). Undeutsch hypothesis and criteria based content analysis: A meta-analytic review. *The European Journal of Psychology Applied to Legal Context, 7*(1), 3–12.

Armistead, T. W. (2011). Detecting deception in written statements: The British Home Office study of scientific content analysis (SCAN). *Policing: An International Journal of Police Strategies & Management, 34*(4), 588–605.

Auburn, T., Drake, S., & Willig, C. (1995). 'You punched him, didn't you?': Versions of violence in accusatory interviews. *Discourse and Society, 6*(3), 353–386.

Baldwin, J. (1993). Police interview techniques: Establishing truth or proof? *The British Journal of Criminology, 33*(3), 325–352.

Brandon, S. E., Wells, S., & Seale, C. (2018). Science-based interviewing: Information elicitation. *Journal of Investigative Psychology and Offender Profiling, 15*(2), 133–148.

Brown, P., & Levinson, S. C. (1987). *Politeness: Some universals in language usage.* Cambridge: Cambridge University Press.

Bull, R. (1989). Can training enhance the detection of deception? In J. C. Yuille (Ed.), *Credibility assessment* (pp. 83–99). Netherlands: Springer.

Bull, R., & Milne, B. (2004). Attempts to improve the police interviewing of suspects. In G. D. Lassiter (Ed.), *Interrogations, confessions, and entrapment* (pp. 181–196). New York: Kluwer Academic.

Cleary, H., & Warner, T. C. (2016). Police training in interviewing and interrogation methods: A comparison of techniques used with adult and juvenile suspects. *Law and Human Behavior, 40*(3), 270.

College of Policing UK. (2018). Investigative interviewing: Principles and ethics. Retrieved from https://www.app.college.police.uk/app-content/investigations/investigative-interviewing/-principles-and-ethics

Cooke, M. (1996). A different story: Narrative versus 'question and answer' in Aboriginal evidence. *Forensic Linguistics: The International Journal of Speech, Language and the Law, 3*(2), 273–288.

Crook, J. R. (2009). President issues executive order banning torture and CIA prisons. *The American Journal of International Law, 103*(2), 331.

DePaulo, B. M., Lindsay, J. J., Malone, B. E., Muhlenbruck, L., Charlton, K., & Cooper, H. (2003). Cues to deception. *Psychological Bulletin, 129*(1), 74.

Eades, D. (1994). A case of communicative clash: Aboriginal English and the legal system. In J. Gibbons (Ed.), *Language and the law* (pp. 234–264). Harlow: Longman Group.

Ekman, P., Friesen, W. V., & Scherer, K. R. (1976). Body movement and voice pitch in deceptive interaction. *Semiotica, 16*(1), 23–28.

Fairclough, N., & Wodak, R. (1997). Critical discourse analysis. In T. A. Van Dijk (Ed.), *Discourse as social interaction* (pp. 258–284). London: Sage.

Garofoli, J. (2018, 9 August). Fearing a trump return to torture, psychologists keep ban at Guantanamo. *San Francisco Chronicle.* Retrieved from https://www.sfchronicle.com/

Gibbons, J. (1996). Distortions of the police interview process revealed by video-tape. *Forensic Linguistics: The International Journal of Speech, Language and the Law, 3*(2), 289–298.

Hartwig, M., Granhag, P. A., & Luke, T. (2014). Strategic use of evidence during investigative interviews: The state of the science *Credibility assessment* (pp. 1–36). San Diego, CA: Elsevier Academic Press.

Hartwig, M., Granhag, P. A., Stromwall, L., Wolf, A. G., Vrij, A., & Af Hjelmsater, E. R. (2011). Detecting deception in suspects: Verbal cues as a function of interview strategy. *Psychology Crime & Law, 17*(7), 643–656. doi:10.1080/10683160903446982

Horvath, F., Blair, J., & Buckley, J. P. (2008). The behavioural analysis interview: Clarifying the practice, theory and understanding of its use and effectiveness. *International Journal of Police Science & Management, 10*(1), 101–118.

International Association of Chiefs of Police. (2018). Training Key #597 assessing witness credibility. Retrieved from https://www.theiacp.org/resources/training-key/597-assessing-witness-credibility

Laboratory for Scientific Interrogation Inc. (n.d.-a). Calendar. Retrieved from http://www.lsiscan.com/id25_the_lsi_basic_course_on_scan.htm

Laboratory for Scientific Interrogation Inc. (n.d.-b). Can you find the confession in this statement? Retrieved from https://www.lsiscan.com/id19.htm

Laboratory for Scientific Interrogation Inc. (n.d.-c). Introduction to SCAN. Retrieved from https://www.lsiscan.com/intro_to_scan.htm

Leal, S., Vrij, A., Mann, S. A., & Fisher, R. P. (2011). Detecting concealed information about person recognition. *Applied Cognitive Psychology, 25*(3), 372–376. doi:10.1002/acp.1701

Linell, P., & Jonsson, L. (1991). Suspect stories: On perspective setting in an asymmetrical situation. In I. Markova & K. Foppa (Eds.), *Asymmetries in dialogue* (pp. 75–100). Hemel Hempstead: Harvester Wheatsheaf.

Meissner, C. A., & Kassin, S. M. (2004). "You're guilty, so just confess!" Cognitive and behavioural confirmation biases in the interrogation room. In G. D. Lassiter (Ed.), *Interrogations, confessions, and entrapment* (pp. 85–106). New York: Kluwer Academic.

Morris, A. (2018). A lie detection expert talks about how to figure out when politicians lie. *Forbes Media LLC.* https://www.forbes.com/sites/andreamorris/2018/08/16/politics-and-lies-insights-from-lie-detection-expert-part-1/

National Research Council. (2003). *The polygraph and lie detection.* Washington, DC: The National Academies Press.

Porter, S., & Yuille, J. C. (1996). The language of deceit: An investigation of the verbal clues to deception in the interrogation context. *Law and Human Behavior, 20*(4), 443–458.

Postma, A. (2000). Detection of errors during speech production: A review of speech monitoring models. *Cognition, 77*(2), 97–132.

Reynolds, E., & Rendle-Short, J. (2011). Cues to deception in context: Response latency/gaps in denials and blame shifting. *British Journal of Social Psychology, 50*(3), 431–449.

Sapir, A. (1987). *The LSI course on scientific content analysis (SCAN).* Phoenix, AZ: Laboratory for Scientific Interrogation.

Scherer, K. R., Feldstein, S., Bond, R. N., & Rosenthal, R. (1985). Vocal cues to deception: A comparative channel approach. *Journal of Psycholinguistic Research, 14*(4), 409–425.

Settle, R. (1990). *Police power: Use and abuse.* Northcote: Muxworthy Press.

Shuy, R. W. (1998). *The language of confession, interrogation and deception.* Thousand Oaks, CA, US: Sage Publications, Inc.

Smith, N. (2001). Reading between the lines: An evaluation of the scientific content analysis technique (SCAN). *Police Research Series, 135.* London, UK: UK Home Office, Research Development and Statistics Directorate.

Snook, B., Eastwood, J., Stinson, M., Tedeschini, J., & House, J. C. (2010). Reforming investigative interviewing in Canada. *Canadian Journal of Criminology and Criminal Justice, 52*(2), 215–229.

Steller, M. (1989). Recent developments in statement analysis. In J.C. Yuille (Ed.), *Credibility assessment* (pp. 135–154). Netherlands: Springer.

Undeutsch, U. (1989). The development of statement reality analysis. In J. C. Yuille (Ed.), *Credibility assessment* (pp. 101–119). Netherlands: Springer.

van Dijk, T. A. (1996). Discourse, power and access. In C. R. Caldas-Coulthard & M. Coulthard (Eds.), *Texts and practices: Readings in critical discourse analysis* (pp. 84–104). London: Routledge.

Vrij, A. (2008). *Detecting lies and deceit: Pitfalls and opportunities*. Chichester, UK: John Wiley & Sons.

Vrij, A., Evans, H., Akehurst, L., & Mann, S. (2004). Rapid judgements in assessing verbal and nonverbal cues: Their potential for deception researchers and lie detection. *Applied Cognitive Psychology, 18*(3), 283–296.

Vrij, A., Granhag, P. A., Mann, S., & Leal, S. (2011a). Lying about flying: The first experiment to detect false intent. *Psychology Crime & Law, 17*(7), 611–620. doi:10.1080/10683160903418213

Vrij, A., Granhag, P. A., Mann, S., & Leal, S. (2011b). Outsmarting the liars: Toward a cognitive lie detection approach. *Current Directions in Psychological Science, 20*(1), 28–32. doi:10.1177/0963721410391245

Vrij, A., Mann, S. A., Fisher, R. P., Leal, S., Milne, R., & Bull, R. (2008). Increasing cognitive load to facilitate lie detection: The benefit of recalling an event in reverse order. *Law and Human Behavior, 32*(3), 253–265.

Williamson, T. (2006). *Investigative interviewing: Rights, research and regulation*. Cullompton: Willan.

Wodak, R. (1996a). *Disorders of discourse*. London: Addison Wesley Longman.

Wodak, R. (1996b). The genesis of racist discourse in Austria since 1989. In C. R. Caldas-Coulthard & M. Coulthard (Eds.), *Texts and practices: Readings in critical discourse analysis* (pp. 107–128). London: Routledge.

Wright Whelan, C., Wagstaff, G. F., & Wheatcroft, J. M. (2014). High-stakes lies: Verbal and nonverbal cues to deception in public appeals for help with missing or murdered relatives. *Psychiatry, Psychology and Law, 21*(4), 523–537.

5 Police cautions and comprehension[1]

Introduction

In jurisdictions with an adversarial justice system, a police interview with a member of the public represents the production of a text that is critical to the future of the lay participant, as well as to the functioning of the various institutions involved. The content of a police interview may lead investigators towards a particular course of action in the investigation; it may be relied upon by lawyers to construct a defence for their client; it may be used by the court to determine a person's innocence or guilt in relation to a crime; and it may influence the sentencing in the case of a guilty finding. The significance of this particular type of institutional interview for the functioning of the criminal justice system has meant that considerable effort is expended in obtaining an accurate record of the interaction (see Chapter 3) and ensuring that police officers clearly communicate to civilians their rights and obligations in relation to police questioning. Without this legal protection, the court cannot be satisfied that the evidence provided by a suspect has not been distorted through coercion. The failure to obtain consent from the suspect or to ensure that they have understood their rights is a common reason for interview evidence to be ruled inadmissible when it is identified by the court (Ehrlich, Eades, & Ainsworth, 2016).

This chapter is specifically concerned with the interactions between police officers and the suspects relating to the suspects' rights and obligations during formal, recorded police interviews. These interactions are critical to the outcome of the police interviews because, as explained above, they have the potential to determine admissibility of the evidence. The suspect's comprehension of the 'caution' text has been of considerable interest to forensic linguistic researchers (Cotterill, 2000; Ehrlich et al., 2016; Gibbons, 1990; Rock, 2007; van Naerssen, 2013) and was the focus of an important document produced by the Communication of Rights Group and endorsed by the International Association of Forensic Linguists in 2015 (Communication of Rights Group, 2015). The document, titled 'Guidelines for Communication of Rights of non-Native Speakers of English in Australia, England and Wales, and the USA,' explicitly addresses the design and delivery of texts used in these countries to advise suspects of their rights because the versions currently used are so linguistically complex that they are easily misunderstood by any but the most fluent of native English speakers. Moreover, these texts are especially difficult to render in another language (i.e. through an interpreter) and as this chapter demonstrates, police officers struggle to communicate the meaning of the rights in plain language to English speakers, let alone produce a version that can be easily translated.

In Victoria, Australia, the communication of rights is shaped by the legislation relating to the conduct of police interviews with suspects contained in the Crimes Act and interpreted for practice in the Victoria Police Regulations, which, at the time that these interviews were recorded, was the text that regulated professional conduct and practice for police officers in Victoria. There are three key texts that are typically read to suspects by the police interviewer. Two are delivered at the beginning of the interview following the identification of the participants: the first is the official caution which informs the suspect of his or her right not to answer questions; the second text informs the suspect of his or her right to legal advice (though not representation in the interview room itself) and to contact with a friend or relative (the 'one phone call'). The third legal text being referred to in this chapter is used by Victoria Police to inform a suspect of their rights and obligations in relation to the taking of fingerprints at the end of an interview after any charges have been laid.

The origins of the three legal texts presented above can be found in the Crimes Act, as mentioned. For instance, the Crimes Act 1958 states in Section 464A(3):

> Before any questioning (other than a request for the person's name and address) or investigation under sub-section (2) commences, an investigating official must inform the person in custody that he or she does not have to say or do anything but that anything the person does say or do may be given in evidence.

The following excerpts demonstrate how these texts can be delivered by a police officer interviewing a suspect. The wording used here is almost identical to the wording used in all the interviews collected by the researcher for an earlier study (Heydon, 2005, 2013).

In the first excerpt, the police officer demonstrates how the first two texts are typically delivered to suspects (Excerpt 5.1).

The third, much longer text is delivered by the same police officer in Excerpt 5.2.

This fingerprinting caution is highly complex, linguistically and conceptually, and is the cause of considerable confusion to suspects. As will be demonstrated in this chapter, the police reliance on the scripted text and unwillingness or inability to migrate the text efficiently from its legal origins to its practical application in the interaction with a suspect results in lengthy delays and miscommunication that has the potential to undermine the admissibility of the interview evidence in the trial.

Excerpt 5.1 Caution given in INT4

1	pio4	okay I'm now going to speak to you john about a burglary
2		but before I do I must inform you
3		that you are not obliged to say or do anything unless you wish to do so
4		but anything you say or do may be given in evidence
5		do you understand that
6	SPT4	Yeah
7	pio4	I must also inform you of the following rights
8		you may contact or attempt to contact a friend or relative
9		to tell that person of your whereabouts
10		you may contact or attempt to contact a legal practitioner
11		do you understand those rights
12	SPT4	yeah
13	pio4	do you wish to exercise any of those rights before the interview proceeds
14	SPT4	Nup
15	pio4	Okay

Excerpt 5.2 Fingerprinting caution delivered in INT4

468	pio4	john you are going to be charged with burglary and theft
469		your fingerprints are required for the purposes of identification
470		your fingerprints may be used in evidence in court
471		if you refuse to give your fingerprints voluntarily
472		a member of the police force may use reasonable force to obtain them
473		if you are not charged with a relevant offense within six months
474		or are so charged but the charge is not proceeded with
475		or you are not found guilty of the offense or any other relevant offense
476		before the end of that period
477		the fingerprints will be destroyed
478		do you understand all this information
479	SPT4	yes
480	pio4	do you wish to comment on any of the information
481	SPT4	no
482	pio4	do you consent to giving your fingerprints here today
483	SPT4	don't worry me ( )
484	pio4	okay the time is ah
485		just on three minutes past ten
486		do you agree
487	SPT4	yes

Approach to the problem

A key difference between police interviews and other forms of institutional discourse is the extent to which there exists a top-down process of recontextualisation (Bernstein, 1990). The actual language used in the police interview is directly influenced, and in some cases prescribed, by legislative requirements of the state, which is a situation unlike a medical consultation or classroom interaction. Indeed, the 'cautioning' of suspects is even unlike other parts of the police interview. For instance, it is quite dissimilar in structure and purpose to the information gathering, where a text in the form of a narrative is produced by the suspect and becomes destined for recontextualisation elsewhere as part of some future courtroom proceedings. The precision of the opening and closing in institutional terms is safeguarded by providing police officers with training and interview aids, such as written forms that guide them through the requisite utterances and are filled out with the suspect's responses as appropriate.

Conversation Analysis (CA) provides a method of exposing the resources used by speakers to construct a coherent conversation, or, in this case, interview. CA practitioners have identified conversational rules that participants adhere to as a way of ordering speaker turns (Sacks, Schegloff, & Jefferson, 1974) and other rules that govern the type of contribution that will be deemed appropriate at any given time (Jefferson, 1984, 1988; Michaud & Warner, 1997; Moerman & Sacks, 1988; Sacks, 1987). While these rules can be broken or amended, they act as a baseline against which conversational norms are measured by participants and marked in the structure and content of the interaction. CA contributes to the methodology of police interview research by enabling the identification of such interactional strategies as question-answer chains (Frankel, 1990), topic initiations and transitions (Button & Casey, 1984; Frankel, 1990; Jefferson, 1984) and formulations (Heritage & Watson, 1979). These strategies can be aligned with the institutional goals and legislative frameworks that shape the discourse, and thus enable the linguistic analysis to be meaningfully applied to the practices of police and lay participants in actual interviews.

Identifying research questions

Given the concern amongst forensic linguists about the complexity of caution texts and the difficulty of communicating rights to a suspect, the analysis of the grammatical features of cautions that create problems for comprehension could form the basis of an interesting classroom or undergraduate research project. In order to further our knowledge in this field of applied forensic linguistic research, however, our questions might rather focus on identifying potential solutions for police practice. For instance, an analysis of police interview data can help us understand the interactional patterns of communication that characterise a suspect's failure to comprehend their rights or a police officer's failure to convey the meaning of the caution text. For the research approach presented in this chapter, the primary research question can be framed as:

> What are the interactional resources that police officers could draw upon to address the problems of miscommunication during the caution?

This, in turn, suggests secondary questions that address the problem at the analytic level, for instance:

a   What are the linguistic characteristics of miscommunication with regard to the caution texts?
b   How can we describe the miscommunication in relation to institutional discourse frameworks?

Data collection

As we will discuss further in Chapter 9, there are a number of sources for police interview data, some of which are publicly available. Court records sometimes include police interview transcripts and this is especially true if there has been a problem with the comprehension of the caution. Of course, if the police interviewing evidence has been ruled inadmissible as a result of the problems with the caution, then it will not be available, but it might appear in the records if the case went to appeal. Some police transcripts are available in the public domain, published by the media, or on social media platforms. For some researchers, police interview recordings or transcripts might be made available by arrangement with the police department or through a community legal service or law firm. Finally, there is the option of reanalysing published transcripts provided by other researchers.[3]

As in Chapter 3, the analysis presented here draws on police interviews recorded in Victoria, Australia and transcribed by the author. The line numbering is from the full interview transcript and thus gives some indication of the position of the excerpts in the interview as a whole.

Data analysis

The first task for our analysis is to identify the linguistic characteristics of miscommunication in the delivery of the caution texts. By way of example, this section presents an analysis of the fingerprinting caution used in the state of Victoria. The analysis, while limited in scope, demonstrates how CA can be applied to describe the interactions precisely in terms of the participants' contributions to the interaction. This helps us to see more clearly where and how the problem of comprehension might occur. One of the most striking features in the data, as we shall see, is that the police interviewers appear ill-equipped to deal with the linguistic challenges that arise when they try to perform this institutional requirement.

The legal texts used by police interviewers to fulfil legislative requirements are most commonly found at the beginning, or Opening, of the interview and at the end, or Closing, of the interview.[2] The Opening of the interview encompasses the identification of the participants, the purpose of the interview, the presentation of the right to remain silent and the right to contact a lawyer and a friend or relative.[3] In the Closing, the charges are laid and the fingerprinting caution is presented. Heydon (2005) presents an analysis of the institutional language used to construct the Opening and Closing phases of the interviews and finds that police officers displayed a reluctance to vary the wording of the legal texts, which, as mentioned above, are based on police regulations and memorised or read out from forms. This contrasts with the situation in England and Wales where officers are required to explain the caution in their own words, or to have the suspects do the same (Rock, 2007, pp. 186–187). Clearly there is an organisational advantage to the former approach as it is intended to minimise the risk that the interview evidence will be ruled inadmissible due to a failure to meet the legislative requirements. However, some examples from the Closure phases of different interviews demonstrate that this inflexibility can contribute to a failure on the part of the interviewing officer to adequately explain the fingerprinting procedure despite evidence that the suspect may not understand certain aspects of the caution.

This phenomenon can be seen clearly in the following excerpt from Interview 8 (hereafter INT8), where a lengthy clarification sequence is undertaken by the participants following the formal request for consent to obtain the suspect's fingerprints. The sequence has been reproduced in full as Excerpt 5.3 and provides a valuable insight into the problems associated with institutional discourse in clarification sequences.

In the above-mentioned excerpt, the suspect, SPT8, indicates that she has not fully understood the caution, by asking very directly in line 472: *so have I got a choice whether I get fingerprinted or not*. SPT8 uses a formulation discourse marker 'so' to indicate that her turn is intended as a request for a summary or conclusion in relation to the prior utterances. In response, however, we see that the police interviewer, pio8, does not offer a relevant second pair part response to her question and instead resumes the question-answer chain of the interview format by asking two further first pair part questions: does she *wish to comment*, and does she *understand*? These questions seem utterly contrary to the Gricean maxim of relation (Grice, 1975), unless we interpret them in light of the police procedure for this caution. In the normal script for this caution, the suspect is asked 'do you wish to comment on this information?' and 'do you understand this information?' Faced with the suspect's spontaneous request for a clarification, the officer pio8 attempts to resume the script, even though his utterances are not valid responses to her question. When she offers a second pair part in line 475, as prompted by pio8's questions, pio8 does not proceed to a clarification, but rather attempts to satisfy SPT8's needs with a repetition of the script. However, SPT8 does not accept this offer, and uses a metadiscoursal comment *I'm just asking you*, prior to clarifying again for pio8 what her question is: *have I got a choice*. In response to this yes/no question, pio8 avoids a binary answer and the 'explanation' he offers is so indirect that SPT8 believes she has a choice not to be fingerprinted, which is not the case.

Pio8 seems aware that a misunderstanding has occurred, but he is apparently unable to address the problem within the scope of the institutional discourse of the Closure phase. In fact, it takes another 51 lines to sort the

84 *Police procedures*

Excerpt 5.3 Fingerprinting caution delivery in INT8

468	pio8:	or you are found not of the offense
469		or any other relevant offense before the end of that period
470		then the fingerprints will be destroyed
471		do you understand this information
472	SPT8:	so have I got a choice whether I get fingerprinted or not
473	pio8:	do you do you wish to comment o- on this information
474		do you understand what I've said to you
475	SPT8:	not really no
476	pio8:	would you like me to read it to you again
477	SPT8:	no I just I'm asking you
478		do d- have I got a choice
479		do I have to be fingerprinted or don't I
480	pio8:	you do you do have a choice
481		you can say you can agree-ee to have your fingerprints taken
482		or you can disagree to have your fingerprints taken
483		(1.7) if you (2.1) disagree to have your fingerprints taken
484		then the poli- then the police can enter into a certain course of action
485		and that's a course of action I've detailed in this ah
486		(0.9) in this ah (0.3) paragraph
487		would you like me to read it to you again
488	SPT8:	no it's okay
489	pio8:	(3.2) do you understand the information which I've read out to you
490	SPT8:	yes
491	pio8:	do you wish to comment on this information
492	SPT8:	(3.2) um (2.1) nah I don't want to be fingerprinted
493	pio8:	you don't want to be fingerprinted
494		oh well that's me next question
495		do you consent to giving your fingerprints
496	SPT8:	no
497	pio8:	you don't
498		all right
499	(sio8):	(do you wa-)
500	pio8:	do you have any reason for not consenting to giving your fingerprints
501	SPT8:	I just don't want to
502	pio8:	okay
503		(2.3) are you aware (1.0) and do you recall me saying during that paragraph
504		that if you refuse to give your fingerprints voluntarily
505		(.) a member of the police force may use reasonable force to obtain them
506		did you hear me say that
507	SPT8:	yeah
508	pio8:	and are you aware of what reasonable force is
509	SPT8:	no

problem out, at which point the suspect, in agreeing to the fingerprinting, states quite succinctly SPT8/560: *yeah I'm not going to be held down* – a clarification which might have occurred some 40 turns earlier if the police interviewer had had access to the resources necessary to construct a more informative explanation. An example from another interview will demonstrate that the comprehension problems in the Closure phase are not restricted to the use of complex legal language and even ordinary words can be misunderstood in this context. Again, the interactional problems become difficult to address within the constraints of the institutional discourse frameworks at play in a police interview.

The interaction presented in Excerpt 5.4 begins with the last part of the statement of the suspect's rights and obligations regarding fingerprinting. As mentioned earlier, in the state of Victoria, the fingerprinting caution is very long and complex even by police standards and it would be reasonable to expect that suspects might not understand every aspect of it. As always, the police interviewer is required to ask the suspect if they understood the caution (as in line 471 above), a question that elicits a negative response quite regularly in the data.

Whereas in Excerpt 5.3 from INT8 the suspect did not understand the meaning of the caution, a different sort of problem arises in this excerpt from INT1.

Excerpt 5.4 Comprehension of fingerprinting caution delivered in INT1

534	pio1:	(0.4) then the fingerprints will be destroyed
535		(0.5) do you understand that information
536	SPT1:	yes I do ((barely audible))
537	pio1:	do you wish to comment on any of this information
538	SPT1:	no
539	pio1:	do you consent to giving your fingerprints
540	SPT1:	no
541	pio1:	(1.5) did you understand this (.) information
542	SPT1:	yep
543	pio1:	(0.6) right I'll just (0.4) read it to you (0.2) again slowly
544	SPT1:	all righ
545	pio1	your fingerprints are required for the purpose of en- identification
546		(0.4) your fingerprints may be used in evidence at court
547		(0.5) if you refuse (.) to give your fingerprints voluntarily
548		(0.2) a member of the police force may use reasonable force to obtain them
549	SPT1:	(0.7) oh right yeah (that's ri-)
550	pio1:	you understand that
551	SPT1:	I understand yeah
552	pio1:	right (0.4) do you consent to giving your fingerprints
553	SPT1:	no I don't
554	pio1:	(0.7) you understand about reasonable force to obtain them
555	SPT1:	yeah
556	pio1:	(0.6) and if you're not charged within six months they get destroyed anyway
557	SPT1:	right (0.9) yep
558	pio1:	(0.3) you understand all that
559	SPT1:	yep
560	pio1:	and you still don't consent
561	SPT1:	(1.0) nah I'll give 'em
562	pio1:	(0.3) oh you do consent
563	SPT1:	ye::ah (.) oh right yeah (.) no look (0.2) yeah I do
564		I'll give 'em no worries

86 *Police procedures*

In Excerpt 5.4, the suspect, SPT1, indicates that he has understood the caution, but when the police interviewer, pio1, requests his consent to undertake the fingerprinting procedure, SPT1 refuses: *no* (line 533). Perhaps because this is not the preferred response (Bilmes, 1988; Sacks, 1987), pio1 seems prepared to negotiate the matter, rather than accept the refusal and proceed to take the fingerprints by force.

In lines 538–541 we can see that pio1, like pio8, has limited resources with which to resolve the problem. As we saw in INT8, the interviewing officer relies heavily on the words and phrases used in the police regulations when attempting to clarify a misunderstanding, whether or not this makes grammatical sense. For instance in line 544, she asks: *you understand about reasonable force to obtain them*. In this way, she does not define any of the terms she is using, but simply checks with SPT1 that he understands them. This approach works no better for pio1 than it did for pio8, and in the end, only a chance expansion of SPT1's negative response (551/SPT1: *nah I'll give 'em*) clarifies the cause of the misunderstanding: SPT1 has apparently interpreted *consent* as something like *object*, and therefore responded negatively, presumably believing he was being compliant.

The clarification produced by pio1 could not have resolved the problem because it did not address the nature of the misunderstanding. Even when faced with the prospect of having to *use reasonable force to obtain* the suspect's fingerprints, pio1 does not attempt to replace the words and phrases of the legal formalities with a significantly less institutional set of terminology, despite being able to recognise that some kind of problem has occurred. In the case described here, the problem is eventually resolved. However, one can well imagine the confusion and aggravation that might have resulted had the misunderstanding not been clarified by the suspect and had the police officers proceeded to use force to obtain SPT1's fingerprints.

Another instance of misunderstanding occurs in INT1 during the process of laying criminal charges (see Excerpt 5.5). Clearly it is of critical importance

Excerpt 5.5 Charging with criminal damage in INT1

497	pio1:	(0.3) um (6.7) hm ⇒ just going to ask you a few more questions
498		you've got um (1.5) you're going to be charged with the assault on Ian
499	SPT1:	right
500	pio1:	and you're also going to be charged with the damage on the door
501	SPT1:	(0.6) I'll pay for the door
502	pio1:	yeah but you understand
503	SPT1:	I mean Betty knows I'll pay for that
504	pio1:	(0.5) but you understand that there's charges pending as well
505	SPT1:	I've already ( )
506	pio1:	(1.0)°ri° (2.1)you're not obliged to say or do anything unless you wish to do so
507		but whatever you do say o-
508		(0.5) whatever you say or do may be recorded and given in evidence
509		you understand that
510	SPT1:	I do

to the admissibility of the evidence that the suspect knows which crimes s/he has been charged with by the police. In Excerpt 5.5, it is unclear whether the suspect believes himself charged with criminal damage (for breaking the shop door), or he believes that he will be charged for the damage in a monetary sense.

In Excerpt 5.5, pio1 seems prepared to proceed to the next stage of the Closing without obtaining a clear confirmation from SPT1 that he understood the nature of the charges made against him. This is a serious failing in the interview process and one that was caused by police assumptions about the interview process which were not shared by the suspect. For instance, pio1's attempt to clarify the charge issue (504/pio1: *(0.5) but you under_stand_ that there's <u>charges</u> pending as well*) does not even use the construction *charged with* that would highlight the criminal meaning of *charge*. Therefore, line 504 can only work as a clarification of her original statement by reference to a structural rule of the interview – that information relating to crime events is not discussed in the Closing. This rule can be described as a type of contextualisation cue (Gumperz, 1982) through which the meaning of the utterance can be understood. By reference to a contextualisation cue such as this rule it becomes evident that the phrase *charges pending* must relate to criminal charges, and not to the financial arrangements between SPT1 and the shop owners as this latter interpretation would be introducing crime event information into the Closing. However, contextualisation cues are not always accessible to both participants and in this case, pio1 is relying on a contextualisation cue for the valid interpretation of her utterance that is not available to SPT1. Without access to the appropriate cues, SPT1 is unable to correctly interpret pio1's clarification.

The discursive practices used by pio1 reveal an assumption underlying the utterance that the suspect will have access to certain institutional knowledge. SPT1, however, appears to be unaware that event information is not being discussed at this point and continues to refer only to the financial meaning of *charges*.

Interpreting data

The analysis of the data samples has demonstrated how it is possible to describe the manifestation of the communication of rights in a police interview. Let us now draw on these findings to respond to the secondary research question b) *How can we describe the miscommunication in relation to institutional discourse frameworks?* Our analysis above revealed turn-taking sequences where police officers ignored the norms of adjacency pair rules and flouted the cooperative principle, mainly the maxim of relation, in order to adhere to institutional scripts. The abnormal turn-taking patterns are a clear sign that police are unable to communicate the suspect's rights within the constraints of the institutional discourse requirements.

88 *Police procedures*

In Chapter 3 we discussed the institutional purpose and goals of police interviews. Although it is common for police to describe the purpose of an investigative interview as the elicitation of a confession (Griffiths & Milne, 2006: 167), the reality is that the organisational goal of the interview is to provide an opportunity for the suspect to provide their version of events in a form that will later be admissible as evidence in court. It is not a search for 'the truth,' nor is it an opportunity to persuade the suspect to change his or her story to reflect some police perception of what may have happened. It is therefore of critical importance that the contributions made to the interview by the suspect are protected from any form of contamination by the police interviewers and the bulk of the legal texts used by police in the course of the interview designed to fulfil this function. The fact that each legal text is followed by some clarification of the suspect's comprehension of the text is a testament to the importance of these texts in the legal process. It is important to emphasise this point because at the heart of this chapter lies the author's contention that, by adhering to police standardised versions of the legal requirements, individual officers run the risk of undermining the admissibility of the interview as evidence because they fail to ensure that the suspects have actually understood their rights. On the other hand, the legal texts must be delivered accurately so that they adequately address the legal requirements of the legislation.

In responding to our primary research question, the findings have demonstrated that *the interactional resources that police officers could draw upon to address the problems of miscommunication during the caution* include a greater autonomy over the wording of the caution. If it were the case that simply reproducing the words of the caution accurately would ensure compliance with the legislation, then repetition, such as attempted in the above-mentioned data excerpts, would be a sound strategy. But the legislation requires that the suspect *understands* their rights, and it is clear that in this regard, the strategy of faithful reproduction will not suffice.[4] If a suspect does not understand the meaning of the caution the first time, the data show that there is a good chance he or she will not gain any enlightenment from hearing the identical phrases a second or third time. What is needed is some interpretation or explanation of the legal phrases, such as that clearly requested by the suspect in INT8 – *so have I got a choice whether I get fingerprinted or not* – when faced with the ludicrous spectacle of two police officers refusing to clarify the meaning of the fingerprinting caution.

To the extent that the police officers are avoiding any re-wording of the caution texts, their capacity to address the miscommunication appears very limited. Police officers need to take on a more expanded role in the process of recontextualising the static legal document produced by state legislature as a 'living' text produced as a result of police-suspect interactions. Our analysis suggests that the process of recontextualisation itself needs to be understood as a more complex task than simple reproduction of a set of phrases. Police officers must be trained to recognise the signs that a legal text is failing to adapt to its new dynamic environment and provide the necessary support in the form of interpretation and explanation. This means that police officers will be given appropriate skill set to become autonomous actors in the communication of rights, utilising a 'professional voice' to negotiate comprehension of the text more effectively.

Applications to legal practice and procedures

As described previously, all police interviews with lay participants are governed to some extent by legal requirements interpreted through police procedures. In the case of interviews with suspects, the procedures that are intended to protect a suspect's rights and inform them of their legal obligations are emphasised in police training manuals and familiarity with these procedures is considered a core aspect of any officer's training and competence. In Australia, the actual legislation relating to police interviewing varies from state to state, but the essential elements are very similar. In Victoria, as mentioned earlier, suspects are informed of their right to remain silent and of their rights to contact a lawyer, a friend or relative, and, when relevant, to have an interpreter present. There are many other interactions that may take place in the course of the interview which are legally defined such as explaining to the suspect about the tape-recording process, making a record of breaks in the interview and making a record of the treatment of the suspect or his/her children by the police. At the end of the interview, there are formal requirements relating to charging the suspect with an offence and an exceptionally long legal text that informs the suspect of their rights relating to fingerprinting. In most of these cases, as discussed in this chapter, police officers are issued with forms or cards that have statements printed on them reflecting the wording deemed most appropriate for the fulfilment of the relevant legal requirements. These statements can be read aloud by the police officer at the appropriate time in the interview and this method is generally held by police officers to be the safest approach to adhering to the legislation and protecting the integrity and admissibility of the evidence gathered in the interview.

Our analysis has demonstrated, however, that the use of these 'cue cards' by police officers can backfire with the potential to irreparably undermine the integrity of the interview evidence. It is at these critical moments that access to a professional police voice – that is to say, an authoritative and perhaps more discretionary approach to the presentation of legal texts in the interview – would provide officers with the level of autonomy needed to judge the extent to which a caution or legal text requires variation in order that the spirit of the law is upheld and the admissibility of the evidence protected.

It is not beyond the capabilities of experts in language and police educators to collaborate on producing guidelines for officers that will ensure both comprehension by suspects and compliance with the legislation. Indeed, there have been a number of instances of alternative approaches to this problem in Australia and overseas, the most common solution being one where suspects are asked to provide their own interpretation of the legal texts and then the police

90 *Police procedures*

interviewer offers a further clarification as required (see for instance Rock, 2007: 258). A radically different approach was developed for multilingual (i.e. interpreter mediated) interviews conducted by the Northern Territory police in Australia, where the caution was recorded being spoken in numerous common Aboriginal languages. The recordings can be played on a digital device during the formal interview, which replaces ad hoc interpretations by an interpreter. In order to create the translations of the cautions in indigenous languages, a front translation was first developed which rendered the legalese of the original English versions into non-technical, plain English. These front translations could be used more widely in Australia as the basis for explanatory texts in monolingual interviews. In short there are a number of innovations developed through linguistic research that seek to introduce a more professional and autonomous role for the police interviewer than is evident in these interviews from the state of Victoria.

Final word

Professor Diana Eades has provided her perspective on the case study in this chapter:

> *Did this suspect understood their rights in this police investigative interview?* I am one of a small group of linguists who are sometimes asked by lawyers to provide an expert linguistic opinion on such a question in a specific case. Of course, we can never be in someone else's mind, but as this chapter has shown, what people say and do in the interaction can provide some clues about likely comprehension.
>
> Close sociolinguistic analysis of the interaction and an understanding of many factors of context are essential to an answer to this question (Eades, 2018). If the person speaks English as a second (or third, fourth...) language, then their English proficiency and the expressions used by police are relevant. While police might think they are mainly using little words, sometimes the grammatical structure of the key sentence is complex: imagine for example lines 3–4 of Extract 1 whizzing by a non-native speaker. And often there is no recognition of the longer time it takes to process something said in a second language.
>
> The extract also shows another common problem: 'may be given in evidence' can be a hard expression to unpack and understand. Non-native speakers with a low proficiency may be misled by the figurative and passive use of the verb 'give' here, also used figuratively in 'I'm required to give you your rights' (which I've heard in some interviews). And the legal expression 'in evidence' (sometimes 'as evidence') has a specific meaning not found in everyday English. Yet this very phrase is central to what is involved in

understanding and deciding whether to invoke the right to silence. That is, 'evidence' here refers to 'information (or story) that a judge or jury uses to decide about a court case.'

The practice of asking suspects to repeat the caution in their own words is an important strategy in helping to reveal what the suspect has understood – it's an example of the paraphrase test of understanding. It is now required police practice in some jurisdictions, although not mandated by law, and it has been recommended by the international group of experts in the guidelines referred to in the introduction to this chapter (Communication of Rights Group, 2015). Several Australian courts have made it clear that when police officers fail to ask suspects to explain the caution in their own words, the admissibility of the interview as evidence may be seriously jeopardised. It is important to point out that while this mainly happens with non-native speakers, research on native speakers' mis/understanding of the caution would lend support to the argument that the 'in-your-own-words' explanation should be required in caution communication with all interviewees, not only non-native speakers.

Linguists have seen some interesting paraphrase attempts from second language speakers, which provide no confidence that the suspect has understood that they don't have to answer the police questions. Factors such as the given limited English proficiency of the suspect, the relative speed and often formulaic style with which this part of the interview tends to be conducted, and the power imbalance between interviewer and interviewee all contribute to such failed explanations. It is not surprising that the 'explain-in-your-own-words' response is often very short and inadequate, inaccurate or incorrect, as the following three examples show:

> 'n- not to talk back' (Eades field notes)
> 'oh- my rights?' (Eades field notes)
> 'If I'm not sc-, scare, I'll do my best, to answer every questions'
> (Cooke, 1996, p. 280)

As the international rights communication group asserts, the use of interpreters is essential in interviews with non-native speakers who cannot correctly, adequately and accurately explain the caution in their own words. And as this chapter has shown, the use of carefully researched and prepared recordings of the caution can be used where practical. Further, with all interviewees, regardless of their proficiency in English, police themselves need to be able to discuss the caution in ordinary English.

Diana Eades,
Professor of Linguistics, University of New England, Australia
Past President of the International Association of Forensic Linguists

Notes

1 This chapter draws on an analysis presented by the author in the edited collection 'Legal-Lay Communication: Textual travel in the legal process.' Heydon, G. (2013). From legislation to the courts: Providing safe passage for legal texts through the challenges of a police interview. In C. Heffer, F. Rock & J. Conley (Eds.), *Legal-Lay communication: Textual travel in the legal process* (pp. 55–77). Oxford: Oxford University Press.
2 For readers familiar with the PEACE structure used in England and Wales, and currently being introduced in some Australian states and in New Zealand, this corresponds to the Engage and Explain phase and the Closure phase (see Chapter 3 in this volume).
3 In the interviews being analysed here the police officers are not trained to build rapport in the Opening as would be the case in jurisdictions where the PEACE structure is used.
4 The Crimes Act (Victoria) 1958 Section 464J (b) clearly places 'the onus on the prosecution to establish the voluntariness of an admission or confession made by a person suspected of having committed an offence.'

References

Bernstein, B. (1990). *Class, codes and control, volume 4 the structuring of pedagogic discourse*. London: Routledge.
Bilmes, J. (1988). The concept of preference in conversation analysis. *Language in Society, 17*, 161–181.
Button, G., & Casey, N. (1984). Generating topic: The use of topic initial elicitors. In J. M. Atkinson & J. Heritage (Eds.), *Structures of social action: Studies in conversation analysis* (pp. 167–190). Cambridge: Cambridge University Press.
Communication of Rights Group. (2015). *Guidelines for communication of rights of non-native speakers of English in Australia, England and Wales, and the USA*. Retrieved from https://lst.org.au/wp-content/uploads/2016/04/Communication-of-Rights.pdf
Cooke, M. (1996). A different story: Narrative versus 'question and answer' in Aboriginal evidence. *Forensic Linguistics: The International Journal of Speech, Language and the Law, 3*(2), 273–288.
Cotterill, J. (2000). Reading the rights: A cautionary tale of comprehension and comprehensibility. *Forensic Linguistics: The International Journal of Speech, Language and the Law, 7*(1), 4–25.
Eades, D. (2018). Communicating the right to silence to Aboriginal suspects: Lessons from West Australia v Gibson. *Journal of Judicial Administration, 28*, 4–21.
Ehrlich, S., Eades, D., & Ainsworth, J. (2016). *Discursive constructions of consent in the legal process*. Oxford, UK: Oxford University Press.
Frankel, R. (1990). Talking in interviews: A dispreference for patient-initiated questions in physician-patient encounters. In G. Psathas (Ed.), *Interaction competence* (pp. 231–262). Washington, DC: University Press of America.
Gibbons, J. (1990). Applied linguistics in court. *Applied Linguistics, 11*(3), 229–237.
Grice, H. P. (1975). Logic and conversation. In P. Cole & J. L. Morgan (Eds.), *Speech acts (Syntax and semantics volume III)* (pp. 41–58). New York: Academic Press.
Griffiths, A., & Milne, R. (2006). Will it all end in tiers? Police interviews with suspects in Britain. In T. Williamson (Ed.), *Investigative interviewing: Rights, research and regulation* (pp. 167–189). Cullompton: Willan.
Gumperz, J. (1982). *Discourse strategies*. Cambridge: Cambridge University Press.
Heritage, J., & Watson, D. R. (1979). Formulations as conversational objects. In G. Psathas (Ed.), *Everyday language: Studies in ethnomethodology* (pp. 123–162). New York: Irvington Publishers.

Heydon, G. (2005). *The language of police interviewing: A critical analysis.* New York: Palgrave Macmillan.

Heydon, G. (2013). From legislation to the courts: Providing safe passage for legal texts through the challenges of a police interview. In C. Heffer, F. Rock & J. Conley (Eds.), *Legal-Ley communication: Textual travels in the law* (pp. 55–77). Oxford: Oxford University Press.

Jefferson, G. (1984). On stepwise transition from talk about a trouble to inappropriately next-positioned matters. In J. M. Atkinson & J. Heritage (Eds.), *Structures of social action: Studies in conversation analysis* (pp. 191–222). Cambridge: Cambridge University Press.

Jefferson, G. (1988). On the sequential organization of troubles-talk in ordinary conversation. *Social Problems, 35*(4), 418–441.

Michaud, S. L., & Warner, R. M. (1997). Gender differences in self-reported response to troubles talk. *Sex Roles, 37*(7/8), 527–540.

Moerman, M., & Sacks, H. (1988). On "understanding" in the analysis of natural conversation. In M. Moerman (Ed.), *Talking culture: Ethnography and conversation analysis* (pp. 180–186). Philadelphia, PA: University of Pennsylvania Press.

Rock, F. (2007). *Communicating rights: The language of arrest and detention.* Houndmills: Palgrave Macmillan.

Sacks, H. (1987). On the preferences for agreement and contiguity in sequences in conversation. In G. Button & J. Lee (Eds.), *Talk and social organisation* (pp. 54–69). Clevedon; Philadelphia, PA: Multilingual Matters Ltd.

Sacks, H., Schegloff, E., & Jefferson, G. (1974). A simplest systematics for the organisation of turn-taking for conversation. *Language, 50*(4), 696–735.

van Naerssen, M. (2013). *The linguistic functions of "knowingly" and "intelligently" in police cautions.* Paper presented at the Bridging the gaps between language and the law. Proceedings of the 3rd European Conference of the IAFL. Porto: Faculdade de Letras da Universidade do Porto.

Part III
Legal process

6 Anonymous reporting of sexual assault

Assessing the value of online, form-based reporting[1]

Introduction

In 2017, the problem of sexual violence against women gained worldwide attention during the high profile case of predatory behaviour and sexual assault perpetrated by Hollywood producer Harvey Weinstein against multiple victims. The subsequent #metoo campaign, where women used the hashtag 'metoo' in social media posts to report their own experiences of mostly unreported or unacknowledged sexual violence and harassment, revealed to the public at large an important fact about sexual violence: most victims never make a formal complaint. This revelation is not new to researchers, who have estimated that 80–90% of sexual assaults are unreported annually (Australian Bureau of Statistics, 2012; Daly & Bouhours, 2010; Johnson, 2012; Rotenberg, 2017).

Reporting sexual assault is a harrowing experience for the victim-survivor or witness (Campbell, 2006; Rich, 2014) and the criminal justice systems of many countries have struggled to create a suitable environment for reporting. The extraordinarily high number of otherwise unreported sexual assaults documented by the #metoo campaign demonstrates that while such offences go unreported to police or other authorities, victim-survivors will disclose their experiences when the conditions are right. Importantly, there is evidence that initial informal disclosure can increase the likelihood of the victim-survivor later making a formal complaint (Heydon & Powell, 2018; Markham, 2015). This chapter examines the language environment that is most appropriate for the disclosure of sexual assault by victim-survivors and witnesses. We will use a linguistic framework to analyse formal and informal reporting options and identify how best to optimise the conditions for disclosure in informal reporting environments such that it might support formal reporting to police leading to prosecution.

Formal reporting options leading to prosecution for sexual assault cases are essentially limited to a police investigation in common law jurisdictions and to police or public prosecution investigation in civil law jurisdictions. A formal complaint might also be made to another authority such as an employer, a union, a human rights organisation or similar body but for a criminal prosecution to proceed, the victim-survivor or witness will be required to provide evidence in the form of an interview with police or prosecution officers.

98 *Legal process*

For many victim-survivors, however, reporting their experiences to police in a formal, on-record interview and continuing to provide evidence through a court trial are too harrowing, embarrassing or risky. Nonetheless, the desire to be heard or to relate their experiences is strongly felt by many victim-survivors and informal disclosure can offer a reporting option that is more accessible and satisfactory than a formal police complaint, even though it is not intended to result in prosecution of the offender. While some police services have developed alternative, anonymous reporting options for victim-survivors of sexual assault, community agencies providing support to victim-survivors have also begun to provide anonymous or confidential reporting services, many using online forms. Similar reporting mechanisms are also being implemented in military bases and university campuses. Other ways in which the internet is used by victim-survivors to report their experiences informally include social media, discussion fora and surveys (Loney-Howes, 2018; O'Neill, 2018; Powell, 2015).

While these informal reporting tools might seem unrelated to formal evidence-gathering, in fact there is evidence to suggest that making an anonymous or confidential report can lead to higher likelihood that the victim-survivor will make a formal complaint (Markham, 2015). It is valid and important, therefore, to consider how informal reporting might best be structured to support any subsequent formal report, whilst still retaining its therapeutic value. This is especially relevant given concerns about the contamination of the evidence and distortions of memory that can occur in an inappropriate questioning environment (see Chapter 3). The research discussed in this chapter focuses on the linguistic features of informal reports that are more likely to support good quality formal reporting.

Approach to the problem

As discussed in Chapter 3, the importance of having a detailed account from a witness to crime in their own words is key to best practice police interviewing (Heydon & Powell, 2018) and protocols such as PEACE in England and Wales (Clarke & Milne, 2001), and the Whole Story Interview in Victoria, Australia (Tidmarsh, Powell, & Darwinkel, 2012) exemplify this narrative-based approach to interviewing. A key concern in this form of interviewing is that the witness's memory is uncontaminated and their account retains its integrity. One aspect of this priority is that a witness provides their account as soon as possible after the event so as to minimise the likelihood that they might hear or see conflicting versions of the events, such as in the media or from bystanders, and inadvertently incorporate external information into their memory. Witnesses can also begin to edit their account in response to social pressure or suggestions from other people about what might have happened (Gabbert, Hope, & Fisher, 2009). For all these reasons, as well as the simple fact that memory deteriorates very quickly, there is a strong preference that the evidential interview takes place immediately and before any other form of reporting such as therapeutic interventions. However, this is not always possible or desirable. Many victim-survivors will require therapeutic interventions that offer support through the formal reporting process. Therefore, we need to ensure that these therapeutic interventions and informal reporting mechanisms are designed to reduce the likelihood of memory distortion or contamination of what might become evidence in a criminal investigation.

This research draws on findings published in 2016 relating to the use of written reporting interview protocols to guide online anonymous and confidential sexual assault reporting services (Heydon & Powell, 2018). That research demonstrated the value of using a written form of the established cognitive interview as the basis for online anonymous or confidential reports. The centrality of the free narrative to the cognitive interview was identified and its value both to the evidential integrity of the report and to the therapeutic value of the process was established. This chapter will extend those findings by considering specific features of an existing reporting mechanism used in Victoria, Australia, and how those features can be analysed as language strategies by participants in an online interaction.

Identifying research questions

As described above, the key problem under investigation here is the design of informal reporting mechanisms that maintain the integrity of the evidence in a victim-survivor's report without threatening the well-being of the reporter. Our overarching research question might therefore be framed as:

> What changes need to be made to the linguistic features of informal reporting tools for anonymous or confidential disclosure of sexual assault to better support a potential police investigation?

In order to analyse the linguistic features of informal reporting mechanisms, we first need to establish the features of the formal interview that might be incorporated into such online tools. One supporting research question might be:

> What are the broad linguistic features of formal, best practice interviews with victim-survivors of sexual assault that are relevant to informal reporting?

A second, more specific, question we might consider to guide our linguistic analysis is:

> What are the question forms or prompts that can be used to elicit narrative responses from users of informal reporting tools?

These questions will allow us to identity the broad linguistic features and specific questions or prompts used in police interviews with victim-survivors that we want to preserve in the online, informal reporting environment.

> While it is beyond the scope of this chapter, the free-form narratives of victim-survivors provided in online discussion forums such as Reddit.com might also provide the basis for linguistic research (cf. O'Neill, 2018). Discourse analytic frameworks such as narrative theory, genre theory, politeness theory or systemic functional linguistics could each provide insights into the ways that users present their experiences in the absence of a questioning structure. Such research might be framed within the same criminological background of sexual assault reporting as used in this chapter, but shift the focus to the language use of participants in the online reporting environment. Provided the researcher has access to relevant data, such research might respond to the following questions:
>
> How are users of online discussion forums and social media presently structuring their narratives in this informal reporting environment?
> Are reports framed from the perspective of the writer as subject, or the offender as subject?
> What is the structure of the narratives produced in reports? Specifically, is a coda (Labov & Waletzky, 1997) used to make sense of the event?
> How is language used to report taboo topics?
> Do the reports exhibit features of genres other than storytelling, such as police reporting or media reporting?
>
> Knowing how victim-survivors use language to report their experiences in an informal environment would be useful to police and policing researchers because it would help to shape the formal questioning format to reflect victim-survivor preferences. For instance, police are assisted by knowing what to expect from victim-survivors, when to offer further prompts and when silence or a change of topic is required.
>
> By combining the findings of such research with the findings of the broader research described in this chapter, we can suggest a design for informal reporting tools that maintains the integrity of the evidence, *and* takes account of the ways in which victim-survivors currently respond to information-seeking questions online.

Data collection

This chapter addresses the linguistic characteristics of questioning design used in online forms, compared to best practice interviewing. The research required to answer the questions set out above can be based on desktop (literature) research and by obtaining online forms used by organisations to collect reports of sexual assault. Prior research has identified several sources for such documents, including government agencies such as the US military, universities and college campuses, and non-government agencies that provide counselling, support and/or advocacy (Heydon & Powell, 2018). Police agencies also provide opportunities for anonymous reporting, such as the Sexual Assault Reporting Option (SARO) and the Alternative Reporting Option (ARO) used by the New South Wales and Queensland state police services, respectively (in Australia). The questions and prompts on the documents or websites used to collect reports can be analysed to establish their linguistic features.

Data analysis

Our first research sub-question focuses on the linguistic characteristics of police interviews that are relevant to informal reporting tools. This question might also be framed as one of register: what are the features of the spoken interview that can be re-produced in a written register? Psychological research into a written form of the cognitive interview by Lorraine Hope, Fiona Gabbert and Ron Fisher resulted in the development of the self-administered interview (SAI) (Gabbert et al., 2009), a paper-based interview questionnaire that has been tested in both laboratory and field conditions (Hope, Gabbert, & Fisher, 2011). The SAI gives us a starting point for our research, as it establishes the features of a written version of the cognitive interview that has been shown to maintain the integrity of the evidence. Two key features of the SAI that relate to language use are the inclusion of instructions to users at the start of the form and the prioritisation of the free-form narrative which includes the avoidance of short-answer questions at the start of the interview. The two features relate to findings from psychological research, but are also supported by linguistic theories of language structure and use.

The inclusion of instructions to users to provide a detailed account is intended to counteract people's natural tendency to be succinct in their responses to questions. In the previous chapter, we discussed the importance of relevance in police interviews: that suspects or witnesses will be compelled to provide relevant responses to questions and this limits what they will include in their answers. We drew on Grice's Cooperative Principle, and in particular the maxim of relevance, as well as the turn-taking structures of ordinary conversation established by Sacks, Schegloff, and Jefferson (1974) to show that participants in an interaction are constrained by conversational norms when they produce responses to first pair parts (e.g. questions). This linguistic insight explains the research findings by Fisher, Geiselman, and Amador (1989) showing that witnesses provided more detailed descriptions of events when they were specifically instructed to 'report everything.' In other words, the experimental research showed that people do not report everything they know unless they are explicitly instructed to do so, and linguistic theory explains why this is the case. Police have always been aware of social or personal reasons why even cooperative witnesses or suspects might not give detailed responses, such as fear of wasting police time or an assumption that the police already know the answers (though this too relates to linguistic theories about pragmatics, and the conversational taboo on presenting known information as new information). Linguistic theory explains why this avoidance of detailed responses can still apply even when the interviewee is a person unlikely to be intimidated by the police environment.

With this in mind, we can determine that a linguistic feature of the formal police interview that is relevant to an online reporting format is the inclusion of specific instructions to users to include as much detail in their responses as they are able.

The third relevant feature that we can draw from the psychology literature on effective police interviewing is that the narrative is not interrupted with police questions that might divert the witness's train of thought. In linguistic terms, this is relevant to the structure of the questions overall, and how the sequence of questions is formed to maintain coherence relative to the interviewee's version of events. The order of questions in a police interview setting is determined by the level of specificity of the required response. Questions that require more specific information from the interviewee are considered inappropriate in the earlier part of the interview, especially before the free narrative has been provided. According to the psychological research, this is for two reasons: first, the narrow questions typically require shorter answers and this can lead the interviewee to conclude that shorter answers are preferred in general; and second, requiring the interviewee to answer specific questions if they are uncertain of the answers might lead them to imagine or fabricate details, inadvertently contaminating their memory of the events. From a linguistic perspective we know that first pair parts, such as questions, strongly compel participants in an interaction to provide a second pair part response, and the Gricean maxim of relation (Grice, 1975) will constrain the response to only that which is relevant, thus reducing the length of the response to a specific question.

From both the cognitive and linguistic perspective, therefore, we have strong evidence that narrowly defined questions need to be avoided until after the free narrative has been elicited.

Our second research sub-question requires an exploration of the actual question forms that might be best suited to the online reporting environment. This is included here because in my own experience as a training provider in police interviewing strategies, a very common question I am asked by police officers is 'what actual questions should I ask?' Extensive research over the last four decades has supported the use of open-ended requests to elicit free narrative responses from interviewees in police interviews (Powell, Fisher, & Wright, 2005). However, the form of the request has not been precisely established. Much of the police interviewing training literature advises officers to use 'TED' questions (a mnemonic for tell, explain, describe). This is consistent with linguistic research demonstrating that TED questions are commonly used by police interviewers with children (Heydon, 2005). The forms 'can you tell me…' and 'can you describe for me…' were found to be especially productive in those circumstances (Heydon, 2007). The features of the more productive questions used in police interviews with children, which might also be useful for a broader vulnerable witness population, were the inclusion of a speech verb ('tell,' 'describe') and the inclusion of the recipient of the talk ('for me'). The politeness marker of the indirect question form 'can you' was also identified as appropriate for the vulnerable witness population. The indirect question was identified as belonging to a less formal register than a direct imperative form such as might be used in a police interview with an adult ('tell me what happened'). The less formal register used in this questioning has also been found appropriate in interviews with vulnerable adults such as victim-survivors of sexual abuse (Powell & Thomson, 1994; Tidmarsh et al., 2012).

Based on this prior research, we can determine that an appropriate prompt to elicit a detailed, free narrative in an online form would ideally include a speech (or writing) verb, indicate the recipient of the report and use a less formal register.

Interpreting findings

The analysis of police interviewing practices within theoretical frameworks about language use reveals several important linguistic features for online informal reporting that will support both therapeutic goals and justice goals of reporting sexual assault. In this section, we will consider how this analysis contributes to the broader research question framed earlier:

> What changes need to be made to the linguistic features of informal reporting tools for anonymous or confidential disclosure of sexual assault to better support a potential police investigation?

We have established that the linguistic features that correlate to best practice police interviewing include:

- specific instructions to users to include as much detail in their responses as they are able,
- an elicitation of the free narrative before any narrowly defined questions,
- an appropriate prompt to elicit a detailed, free narrative which includes a speech (or writing) verb, indicates the recipient of the report and uses a less formal register.

In order to respond to the research question, however, we need to also consider the current practices used by online reporting tools. In Victoria, Australia, the South Eastern Centre Against Sexual Assault hosts a reporting website called Sexual Assault Reporting Anonymously (SARA). The SARA form, according to an analysis provided by Heydon and Powell (2018), is one of the best examples of a client-focused system for confidential online reporting of sexual assault. There is an opportunity for the user to provide a narrative response to the question: 'Tell us what happened' under a heading 'About the incident.' The form also includes several free-text fields for information that might otherwise be captured using a closed format such as the description of the offender and the location. This means that users can provide detailed descriptions of these items when simple descriptive terms are inadequate to capture the user's experiences or memories. Nonetheless most of the questions on the form are prefaced by closed questions, or simply headings, for instance 'Offender height.' The main narrative report, mentioned above, is placed at the end of the form, which, according to the research, does not maximise the likelihood that the user will provide a detailed narrative (Milne & Bull, 1999).

Three other reporting mechanisms available online in Australia each follow the same format, using mainly tick boxes and short-answer questions with a request for a narrative at the end of the form. These examples include the two police agency forms mentioned above (SARO and ARO) and the Sexual Assault Disclosure form used by an advocacy organisation Queensland Bravehearts Inc, which does not request a narrative per se, except for a question 'Any other information you would like to add.' These four reporting mechanisms are, to date, the only available sexual assault written reporting tools in Australia.

Forms used by university colleges in the United States for anonymous reporting of incidents typically provide little or no space for a narrative account, and only use closed questions with specific responses in the form of check boxes. Heydon and Powell find that none of the forms available for reporting in the US colleges include cognitive interviewing strategies that might assist respondents to recall details, but rather 'every form presented its requests for information in a format that utterly contradicts the findings of the last four decades of empirical research into witness interviewing questioning protocols' (2018, p. 640)

Applications to legal practice and procedures

While the three items on this list might appear straightforward to implement, the precise wording that maximises narrative detail and minimises contamination of the evidence might require some testing in a laboratory or experimental environment. The therapeutic value of reporting also needs to be taken into consideration – indeed it is of utmost importance – and any questions that are used must be appropriate to the therapeutic goals of the participants. Instructing users of the online reporting tool to provide details can suggest to some victim-survivors that their inability to recall details undermines the validity or credibility of their story. It might be true that, for evidential purposes, a very detailed witness account is usually required, but when the goal is primarily therapeutic, any disclosure is a valid engagement with the support agency that provides an opportunity for the victim-survivor to be offered counselling. Therefore, the instruction that is used needs to be carefully constructed to achieve these somewhat conflicting goals. For example, users might be told that:

> You are welcome to provide as much detail as you are able to recall. We encourage you to write about any and all aspects of your experience that are important to you. Even if you only recall part of what happened, you can write about whatever you can remember.

It might be possible to use such a text in place of the main request for a narrative. If a separate prompt is required, it might echo some of these linguistic properties. For example, the following prompt could be placed above an expanding text box:

> Please use the space below to tell us as much as you can recall about what happened.

Placing specific questions after the elicitation of the narrative might cause some users to feel that they are repeating themselves, or even that they included details in the 'wrong place' if the answers to the specific questions were included in their free narrative. Speakers (and writers) are especially sensitive to being asked to repeat information and it is usually interpreted as a suggestion that they have not told the truth, or that they gave an incorrect response. It is therefore important that the specific questions are prefaced by a brief explanation about their purpose and that users are reassured that it is acceptable for them to repeat information already contained in their free narrative. For example, the free narrative box might be followed by the following text:

> Thank you for telling us your story. We would like to ask you for some specific information now. Although you might already have included this information in your story, it would be helpful if you could provide this information here as well.

In order to test these prompts and instructions, it might be possible to create a beta testing website for users to explore. Working with a service provider, the forensic linguistic researcher can suggest various texts for prompts and instructions and analyse the responses to different versions of the online form. Some of the analyses suggested in the boxed text above might be useful at this evaluative stage of the research. A user survey might also be conducted; however within this environment it can be difficult to implement a survey that does not interfere with the therapeutic goals of the service provider.

Final word

Associate Professor Anastasia Powell is a high profile criminologist working on the cutting edge of digital criminology. Working with massive online data sources, such as Twitter feeds and web forum contributions, she provides a valuable perspective of the role of linguistics in criminological research.

> Criminologists and legal scholars have long critiqued the limitations of traditional criminal justice processes for providing 'justice' for victim-survivors of sexual violence. More than measured merely by a guilty verdict however, for many victim-survivors it is having the opportunity first to disclose what happened in their own words and second, to have that account heard and validated, that represents some of the important elements of justice 'being done' (Clark, 2015; Herman, 2005). Yet criminal justice processes from online reporting forms, to police interviews, to written statements, and all the way to giving testimony in court appear, to paraphrase Judith Herman (2005), to have been designed as the antithesis of providing victim-survivors this very opportunity. What then might the disclosures of victim-survivors
>
> *(Continued)*

look like, when they are provided with this opportunity? How might their experience of 'justice' be improved? And what outcomes might ensue both for societal understandings of sexual violence, and indeed, courtroom understandings in particular? Analysing the narrative disclosures of sexual violence victim-survivors in online and other fora provides a unique perspective from which to explore these questions and indeed develop new possibilities for achieving justice.

Among the challenges for criminologists, however, is the development of new tools suitable for the analysis of such big textual data sets. While 'big data' analytics have developed to enable us to interrogate the when, where, and even broad sentiment of content, there has, to date, been little criminological engagement with how to analyse textual big data more deeply. The further development of such methodological tools would be an enormous contribution to the rapidly emerging field of digital criminologies (Powell, Stratton, & Cameron, 2018). In general terms, digital criminologies represent both a call to engage conceptually with questions of crime, justice and inequality in a digital society; and to engage empirically with questions regarding appropriate methods and ethical concerns in researching digital society. To do the latter will require interdisciplinary collaborations with fields of linguistics, computer sciences and criminologies, which currently are rarely to be found.

Anastasia Powell
Associate Professor of Criminology, RMIT University, Australia
Co-convenor, Gendered Violence and Abuse Research Alliance

Note

1 This chapter draws on data collected for a research project conducted with the South Eastern Centre Against Sexual Assault (Victoria, Australia) with approval from the RMIT University Human Research Ethics Committee. I wish to acknowledge the contributions of the co-investigator Associate Professor Anastasia Powell, research assistant Dr Rachel Loney-Howes and the Gendered Violence and Abuse Research Alliance, RMIT University, in establishing the criminological framework for that research.

References

Australian Bureau of Statistics. (2012). *Personal safety survey* (Catalogue No. 4533.0). Retrieved from Canberra https://www.abs.gov.au/ausstats/abs@.nsf/Lookup/by%20Subject/4533.0~2018~Main%20Features~Personal%20Safety%20Survey~24

Campbell, R. (2006). Rape survivors' experiences with the legal and medical systems: Do rape victim advocates make a difference? *Violence Against Women, 12*(1), 30–45.

Clark, H. (2015). A fair way to go. In N. Henry, A. Powell, & A. Flynn (Eds.), *Rape justice: Beyond the criminal law* (pp. 18–35). London: Palgrave Macmillan.

Clarke, C., & Milne, R. (2001). *National evaluation of the PEACE investigative interviewing course*. London: Home Office, UK

Daly, K., & Bouhours, B. (2010). Rape and attrition in the legal process: A comparative analysis of five countries. *Crime and Justice, 39*(1), 565–650.

Fisher, R. P., Geiselman, R. E., & Amador, M. (1989). Field test of the cognitive interview: Enhancing the recollections of actual victims and witnesses of crime. *Journal of Applied Psychology, 74*, 291–297.

Gabbert, F., Hope, L., & Fisher, R. P. (2009). Protecting eyewitness evidence: Examining the efficacy of a self-administered interview tool. *Law and Human Behavior, 33*(4), 298–307.

Grice, H. P. (1975). Logic and conversation. In P. Cole & J. L. Morgan (Eds.), *Speech acts (syntax and semantics volume III)* (pp. 41–58). New York: Academic Press.

Herman, J. L. (2005). Justice from the victim's perspective. *Violence Against Women, 11*(5), 571–602.

Heydon, G. (2005). *The language of police interviewing: A critical analysis*. New York: Palgrave Macmillan.

Heydon, G. (2007). The importance of being (in)formal. In K. Kredens & S. Goźdź-Roszkowski (Eds.), *Language and the law: International outlooks* (pp. 279–303). Frankfurt Am Main: Peter Lang GmbH.

Heydon, G., & Powell, A. (2018). Written-response interview protocols: An innovative approach to confidential reporting and victim interviewing in sexual assault investigations. *Policing and Society, 28*(6), 631–646. doi:10.1080/10439463.2016.1187146

Hope, L., Gabbert, F., & Fisher, R. P. (2011). From laboratory to the street: Capturing witness memory using the self-administered interview. *Legal and Criminological Psychology, 16*(2), 211–226.

Johnson, H. (2012). Limits of a criminal justice response: Trends in police and court processing of sexual assault. In E. Sheehy (Ed.), *Sexual assault in Canada: Law, legal practice and women's activism* (pp. 613–634). Ottawa: University of Ottawa Press.

Labov, W., & Waletzky, J. (1997). Narrative analysis: Oral versions of personal experience. *Journal of Narrative & Life History, 7*(1-4), 3–38.

Loney-Howes, R. (2018). Shifting the Rape script:"Coming Out" online as a Rape victim. *Frontiers: A Journal of Women Studies, 39*(2), 26–57.

Markham, C. J. (2015). Restricted reporting on California military installations: The unnecessary and unwise state law exception. *Harvard Law School National Security Journal*. Retrieved from http://harvardnsj.org/2015/01/restricted-reporting-on-california-military-installations-the-unnecessary-and-unwise-state-law-exception/-_edn5

Milne, R., & Bull, R. (1999). *Investigative interviewing: Psychology and practice*. Chichester; New York: Wiley.

O'Neill, T. (2018). 'Today I Speak': Exploring how victim-survivors use reddit. *International Journal for Crime, Justice and Social Democracy, 7*(1), 44–59.

Powell, A. (2015). Seeking rape justice: Formal and informal responses to sexual violence through technosocial counter-publics. *Theoretical Criminology, 19*(4), 571–588.

Powell, A., Stratton, G., & Cameron, R. (2018). *Digital criminology: Crime and justice in digital society*. New York: Routledge.

Powell, M., Fisher, R. P., & Wright, R. (2005). Investigative interviewing. In N. Brewer & K. Williams (Eds.), *Psychology and law: An empirical perspective* (pp. 11–42). New York: The Guildford Press.

Powell, M., & Thomson, D. M. (1994). Children's eyewitness-memory research: Implications for practice. *Families in Society: The Journal of Contemporary Human Services*, April, 204–215.

Rich, K. (2014). *Interviewing rape victims: Practice and policy issues in an international context*. Houndsmill: Palgrave Macmillan.

Rotenberg, C. (2017). Police-reported sexual assaults in Canada, 2009 to 2014: A statistical profile. *Juristat: Canadian Centre for Justice Statistics, 37*(1). Statistics Canada Catalogue no. 85-002-X.

Sacks, H., Schegloff, E., & Jefferson, G. (1974). A simplest systematics for the organisation of turn-taking for conversation. *Language, 50*(4), 696–735.

Ticmarsh, P., Powell, M., & Darwinkel, E. (2012). Whole story: A new framework for conducting investigative interviews about sexual asault. *II-RP Journal, 4*(2), 35–44.

7 Legal investigative interviewing

Questioning strategies in civil and administrative investigations

> In my capacity as an academic staff member working in a busy criminology and justice department at RMIT University in Melbourne, I deliver regular undergraduate units on investigative interviewing which I sometimes provide as short courses to investigators seeking professional development. Following one such short course, I was approached by a group of attendees from a Regulatory Compliance Branch (RCB) of a large government commission. They had enjoyed the short course and were keen for me to deliver on-site training to their whole unit. I said 'no.' They seemed a bit surprised – I probably could have delivered the response less emphatically, now I think about it – but I explained that while I could come and deliver the material to their staff, I did not think it was the best use of my time and their money. What they needed was not yet another off-the-shelf police interviewing training course; what they needed was a research project. I proposed, and they enthusiastically agreed to, a model whereby I would conduct a data gathering activity with them, and design a set of training modules based on their specific needs. It must have sounded like a pretty standard consultancy proposal, but in conversation with the investigators, I was able to demonstrate the value of linguistic insight to the project that only a forensic linguist might offer. For instance, one of the first things that they mentioned was how spending cuts had reduced their travel budget and, given that Australia is a very big country similar in size to the United States, this had prevented them from flying to the interstate investigation sites and they were now conducting many of their interviews over the phone. They were also making use of video conferencing technology when it was available. This immediately brought to my mind the problem of receipt markers for interviewers: verbal markers such as 'yes' or 'right' are generally used by listeners to indicate 'receipt' of a speaker's turn, especially during a storytelling event. However, such receipt markers can indicate *agreement* for some speakers (more typically men), and so many interviewers prefer non-verbal receipt markers. They nod slowly, or lean forward to show attentiveness. But telephone and video conferencing technologies introduce conflicting requirements: on the phone, a verbal indicator is crucial

(*Continued*)

110 Legal process

to signal that the call is still 'live,' and even in video conferencing it can be hard to position the camera so that all parties are clearly visible to each other, so gestures and non-verbal indicators are similarly unreliable. How then can interviewers use verbal indicators without suggesting that they agree with everything the witness is saying? That I was able to articulate the problem so precisely for the investigators was greatly reassuring for them. This was something that even experienced face-to-face interviewers had been struggling with in the new mode of communication and yet they could not put their finger on what was going wrong. We didn't come up with a solution then and there, but we were able to include the receipt marker problem in the project and consider the implications of what might have seemed a trivial detail to a non-linguist.

Here I will draw on the findings of that project and a similar project conducted with tribunal members reviewing claims for asylum. I will demonstrate how research translation can maximise the impact of forensic linguistics research for legal professionals and ultimately society at large.

Introduction

In previous chapters we have drawn primarily on the literature from pragmatics and conversation analysis to demonstrate the application of theories about turn-taking, topic management and conversational implicature to the analysis of police interviewing (Chapter 3) and online report gathering (Chapter 6). In this chapter we will move to a wider lens and consider the kind of research that might enable a professional community to improve their interviewing practices. At the heart of such improvements we will still find the application of pragmatics and sociolinguistics, alongside the interviewing research from cognitive psychology, which has largely shaped the way modern police interviewing is conducted. However, the issue we are exploring through our research is not simply the best way to ask questions, but more broadly, the best way to develop and deliver training for professional investigators. This might seem a long way from the accepted definition of 'forensic linguistics' and yet, apart from expert testimony, the impact of forensic linguistic research is most easily identifiable and measurable through training that delivers the findings in an applied setting. It is therefore important to include an exploration of training development in this volume, since it is by far the most common means by which forensic linguistic research is translated into social or institutional impact.

Approach to the problem

For this type of research, the questions are focused on how a specific investigative environment might benefit from academic knowledge about interviewing. The data sources for the project will be drawn from the investigative environment itself, and set within a context of the primary research relevant to interviewing such as pragmatics, sociolinguistics and conversation analysis. The body of research from cognitive psychology that underpins investigative interviewing training will not be ignored either. As in previous chapters, the linguistic findings about how interview participants negotiate the production of their verbal contributions will be considered within a framework of established best practice interviewing skills, such as rapport building, eliciting a free narrative and using appropriate questions to avoid contaminating the interviewee's story.

This research is important because many organisations and branches of government engage in interviewing within a legal framework. There are tribunals, commissions, enquiries and review boards conducting investigative interviews that affect the lives and livelihoods of many more citizens than would ever be questioned by police. And yet, there is very little research that exists to guide these organisations in their interviewing practices. Apart from recruitment interviewing, little attention is paid to the practices of investigative interviewers in non-police environments. For example, a peer-reviewed article offering advice to health care managers conducting workplace investigations provides a number of suggestions about conducting an interview, but does not cite any literature or research findings to support the suggestions that are made (Mitchell & Koen, 2012). This is not to say that the suggestions are invalid, but the use of these specific strategies is not supported with any empirical evidence that they work.

We can help to close this gap through research projects involving a range of investigative environments. This chapter presents two projects that addressed the needs of investigators conducting interviews in non-police environments. Rather than focus on the findings of these projects, this chapter will set out the approach to the data gathering and analysis, and describe some of the techniques used to provide training to the professional staff so that they might engage meaningfully in the process and contribute to the development of the materials. This was substantially more successful in one project than the other, and so a comparison of the training development and delivery is also provided to see why this might have been so.

Project 1 – RCB

The first project, referred to in the boxed text at the start of the chapter, involved the RCB of a national workplace investigation commission in Australia. The RCB had previously engaged a police officer to deliver interviewing training and this included advice about things like protecting one's personal safety by ensuring the suspect was not seated between the interviewer and the door. According to the participants in the project, their prior training did not include advice about how best to conduct an interview over the phone nor was it tailored to help them to manage their own legislative requirements effectively.

Project 2 – RRT

The second project involved the Refugee Review Tribunal (RRT). The RRT was established in 1993 in order to provide an independent review of decisions made by the Department of Immigration and Border Protection (DIBP) about an

112 Legal process

asylum seeker's application for protection. The RRT is structured, as are many tribunals, in a less formal manner than other areas of justice. The hearings themselves do not follow a strictly structured procedure and are non-adversarial by nature. Under s 420.2(a) of the *Migration Act 1958* (Cth), the RRT 'is not bound by technicalities, legal forms or rules of evidence.'

Within this more informal structure, the hearing takes place in a rather ordinary room with a large desk acting as the Bench, and the presiding decision-maker is referred to as the Member. Members had usually received some professional development training about cross-cultural communication and working with an interpreter, and, like the investigators of the RCB, they had undertaken training specific to their workplace, but unlike at the RCB, the training had not addressed interviewing skills.

Identifying research questions

These projects require a qualitative method that will best achieve the goals of the research. In terms of research design, these projects are best described as case studies, since they involve the detailed study of a single unit at a point in time, although they also draw on elements of ethnographic research, to the extent that they utilise narratives, texts and observation to describe the working culture and practices of a group. Additionally, there can be some elements of participatory action research, where the individuals who make up the 'unit' under consideration are themselves involved in researching their own experiences and practices (e.g. of investigative interviewing). This can occur in the delivery of training, as will be discussed below.

This is highly applied, consultative research that involves an iterative process of generating research questions, gathering data from the first available source, analysing the findings of those data and refining the research questions to apply to the next data source. In the research methodological literature, this process has been called progressive focusing (Parlett & Hamilton, 1972) and using this method, '[i]nitial research questions may be modified or even replaced in mid-study by the case researcher. The aim is to thoroughly understand [the case]. If early questions are not working, if new issues become apparent, the design is changed.' (Stake, 1995, p. 9). Nonetheless, it is still possible to set out research questions that need to be answered in the process of the research as a whole. The following are three such questions, but note that in the process of the individual research projects, several others presented themselves for investigation.

1   How does the investigative environment of the RCB or the RRT affect the conduct of interviewers and interviewees during the interview or questioning procedure?
2   Are there specific factors affecting these investigations such that the strategies taught in typical police investigative interviewing courses are ineffective or inappropriate for use by the RCB or RRT investigators?

3   What are the most effective strategies for interviewing in each of these environments? In particular, are there new strategies for Engage and Explain, topic management and/or presentation of evidence phases that might work more effectively in these interviews, especially telephone interviews (RCB) or interviews that involve an interpreter (RRT)?

Data collection

In both projects, the problem could be approached by triangulating several different sources of information in order to identify gaps and inconsistencies that required attention. The sources have been grouped into three categories and described as follows:

A. Regulations and legislation

Both organisations were governed by regulatory regimes and both were investigating cases that would require decisions or recommendations based on an interpretation of the law. The starting point in both projects was to conduct research into the relevant regulations and legislation governing the investigators' practices.

B. Investigator knowledge and behaviour

The next important source of data was the investigators themselves. What were their experiences of working within the legislative or regulatory framework and what were the questioning strategies that they were currently using? There are three main ways of eliciting data from the investigators. First, researchers can conduct direct observation of live or recorded interviews. In the examples used here, some limited real time observation was possible in the RRT and supplemented with observations of hearings in the related Migration Review Tribunal (MRT).[1] This was not possible in the RCB, and no recordings of interviews were available from either setting. In Chapter 9 of this book, we discuss methods of effective data gathering through observation alone when electronic recording is not possible. One of these is the Labovian model of quantifying the manifestation of a small number of variables as they occur in real time (Labov, 2006). This method was used in the RRT and MRT hearings to collect data relating to question types according to the cognitive interviewing model, which is a suitable variable with a limited number of possible variants (open TED prompt, closed WH-questions, binary yes/no questions, appropriate why questions, inappropriate why questions, multiple questions, forced choice questions, leading questions, tag questions, misleading questions, statements/opinions). It is a particularly useful method in forensic linguistic research because of its application in environments where electronic recording is prohibited, but the data are otherwise publicly accessible such as many court and tribunal hearings.

Second, field interviews with the investigators can be conducted to elicit information such as self-reported behaviours and attitudes or beliefs about interviewing. In these interviews, it is important not to contaminate your data with leading questions – indeed, the very skills you are seeking to identify in your participants must be present in your own interviewing method. For field interviews, I generally use a very broad set of questions to elicit narrative-based responses, and support the findings with information from questionnaires or desktop research, such as the regulatory or legislative documents mentioned above, or training materials (see below). The questions used to interview participants in both projects were adapted from Dando, Wilcock, and Milne (2008) and cover the following areas:

1. background information about the investigators (e.g. age, length of service and general duties),
2. interviewing experience (the number of investigative interviews or hearings they conduct each week and types of investigations they involve),
3. interview techniques (the way the investigators elicit information from informants/applicants),
4. impressions of interviewing (whether they had ever felt pressured when interviewing subjects and what types of pressure they experienced),
5. operational experiences (e.g. note-taking and recording interviews, conducting telephone/Skype interviews),
6. training experiences (whether their training had equipped them with necessary skills to interview effectively in the RCB/RRT environment; whether skills learned in police interviewing courses were transferable to the RCB/RRT environment).

Data from the interviews were analysed in two ways i.e. simultaneous and inductive. In the former, data are analysed on an ongoing basis. That is, while data are collected, the researcher simultaneously seeks to capture in their notes the general statements from the participants. This way 'allows for ideas to emerge from the data as they are collected' (Minichiello, Aroni, & Hays, 2008, p. 259). In the case of the latter, data from interviews are transcribed, broken into manageable units and coded based on common themes or propositions (Minichiello et al., 2008).

Third, in addition to the field interviews and/or observations, researchers can use questionnaires or tests to gather data about attitudes, beliefs and skills relating to interviewing. This strategy was used in the RCB project, which greatly assisted the analysis and also provided an opportunity to ensure that all the participants in the training began with similar background knowledge about key interviewing theories and concepts. The key to this outcome was to design an online test that provided extensive technical explanations and definitions as background to the actual questions, and then used the questions to test the participant's understanding of or attitude towards the information provided. The screenshot in Figure 7.1 provides an example of what one of the introductory questions looked like.

Q3 What is Investigative Interviewing?

In policing, it is common for the term 'interviewing' to be applied only to the interviewing of suspects. It is important to remember however that investigative interviewing includes the interviewing of witnesses and victims, and outside of policing, we require techniques that can be applied to a range of interviewees. Sometimes this means that the terminology or strategies that are used in police-based training are not quite appropriate for other environments, but generally the underlying principles are sound. This is especially true of investigative interviewing which is now an internationally recognised term. It does not relate only to police interviews and there are now quite a few private companies that provide training on investigative interviewing to a range of organisations, although this course is the first to be specifically tailored to the unique ▮▮▮ RCB environment.

An interview has been described as "a conversation with a purpose." What then do you think is the purpose or goal of investigative interviewing?

In policing, it is common for officers to say that the main purpose is "to elicit a confession." Perhaps you also feel this is the main purpose of some of your interviews, although you might not use the term 'confession', but something similar. If this is your answer take a moment to think about the implications of that statement. It implies not only that you think of interviews as predominantly with "suspects" but that you already know that your suspect is guilty. In some cases you might have a strong suspicion but you should never assume guilt when conducting an interview.

"The goal of investigative interviewing is to collect reliable data to be used for informed decision making and taking just actions."

Take a moment to think about this statement and indicate below whether you agree with the benefits of displaying open mindedness.

○ Strongly agree
○ Agree
○ Somewhat agree
○ Neither agree nor disagree
○ Somewhat disagree
○ Disagree
○ Strongly disagree

Figure 7.1 Screenshot of questionnaire used with RCB group.

C. Training materials

A further data source is any existing training materials or interviewing guidelines provided to investigators. In some cases, this might not differ greatly from the regulations mentioned earlier, and this in itself is useful to know because it can indicate a lack of resources dedicated to interviewing training. When reviewing training materials and regulations, it can be helpful to undertake a directed analysis guided by the previous data analysis. For instance, if there are specific language requirements that are mentioned by the participants in the interviews, or you observe specific language behaviours in situ (e.g. in observing court hearings), you might be able to confirm whether or not such behaviours have their origin in formal training guidelines.

Data analysis

There is not the space here to present a comprehensive description of the data analysis in each of the two projects. However, it is possible to set out the analytical methods that were applied to each of the data sets, and provide some indicative analyses by way of example.

Beginning with the desktop research indicated above in Section A, *Regulations and legislation*, researchers will need to identify aspects of the text most relevant to investigations. Depending on the volume of materials, it may mean that researchers need to target their review of the text using search tools and indices. As a starting point, researchers might identify keywords such as 'interview,' 'investigate,' 'evidence' and 'statement' which can be used as search terms in very large documents. Additionally, text that mentions electronic recording or note-taking is likely to be related to interviewing. Analytical tools that can be applied here include any application that allows text searching, ranging from a web browser to a qualitative data analysis application such as Nvivo, Atlas ti or similar programs. Note that these programs are designed for complex coding and sorting operations that might not be as important at this stage, but might be useful when analysing other data, especially interview data.

The main objective of the analysis of the legislation and regulations data is simply to describe the legal constraints within which the investigators are required to conduct an interview. These documents will most likely state the means by which the unit derives its powers (usually through an Act of government) and sets out: the powers of arrest or detainment, if any; the powers to compel evidence (i.e. require a person to answer questions or require documents, including electronic files, to be provided to the investigators); and the types of offense that can be investigated and those cases that need to be referred to another agency. It might also be possible to identify the qualifications required by investigators. This is important because, in some cases, the prior experience of the investigator might influence their approach to interviewing. For example, Members of the RRT tended to have legal backgrounds but this was not a pre-requisite and some Members had prior roles as professionals with some tribunal or review board function. This meant that individual Members brought very different skills sets and professional approaches to their role as interviewer in a hearing. Having this information in advance ensured that the data gathering interviews included questions about prior experience and training in conducting investigations or hearings.

Moving on to Section B, *Investigator knowledge and behaviour*, the data to be analysed here are predominantly interview data, but included observation materials from the RRT/MRT hearings in that project. When analysing these text data, it is useful to keep in mind that in addition to the primary message content, we are also interested in the evaluative attitude of the speaker towards the message. We might also need to keep track of whether the content of the interviewee's response is expressing the participant's individual concern, or whether it is intended to be representative of the team's shared concerns. It is also useful to note whether the participant is discussing an actual case or experience, or whether they are providing a hypothetical example. These aspects of the data can be coded during the analysis, although this is not usually a productive framework for interpretation of results in and of itself. Nonetheless, identifying substantial differences between what an individual identifies as their own experiences of interviewing and what they describe as the group's experience of interviewing might provide insights to probe with other interviewees. For example, in the RCB project, it became clear as the field interviews progressed that participants would say that as individuals they felt that their previous experience (mostly paralegal/administrative work) had not prepared them for the confrontational aspects of their investigations, where subjects of an investigation might become aggressive or upset while being questioned. However, none of the interviewees identified this issue as concerning the group more broadly: they interpreted it as a personal failing rather than seeing it as a gap in their training that could be rectified by the organisation.

Returning to the data analysis more generally, it will be necessary to decide on an approach to the coding of the data. What I have described in this chapter is best suited to Framework Analysis, which involves identifying an initial coding framework of themes from a priori issues, such as those identified in the legislative and regulations review, and from emergent issues such as the example given above about participants' preparedness for managing difficult or aggressive subjects. The next stage of the analysis will involve attaching codes to the pieces of data that correspond to different themes. This can be undertaken manually or it can be semi-automated using one of the qualitative data analysis software packages designed for this purpose.[2]

Following the coding process, and depending on the software or manual process used, the coded segments can be charted using headings from the thematic framework. In the RCB and RRT projects, a heading such as 'Current interview techniques' would represent a theme based on the field interview question schedule (see above). Under this heading, we would gather all the segments coded for 'interviewing techniques,' either by copying the segments manually into a spreadsheet or list, or by using the coding and analysis functions of a software package.

The next stage of the Framework Analysis involves interpreting the coded data by searching for patterns, associations, concepts and explanations. To continue the example given above, the segments that are gathered together under the heading 'Current interview techniques' could be further sorted according to the code 'participant's attitude.' In the RCB project, the interview data were coded for 'participants' attitude to content' using a simple three point scale with the range: 'broadly supportive' – 'neutral' – 'broadly critical.' By mapping the segments coded and collected under the theme 'Current interview techniques' against the codes for 'attitude' patterns emerged showing which interviewing techniques were viewed positively by the participants and which were viewed critically, and how consistent these attitudes were between participants. One clear pattern to emerge was the consistency of dissatisfaction with police

118 *Legal process*

training. Another, more surprising, finding was the inconsistency of attitudes towards telephone interviewing: some participants strongly resented the reliance of the RCB on remote interviewing as a cheap alternative to on-site interviews, and my early interactions led me to expect this to be a universal belief amongst RCB investigators. But the data mapping exercise instead demonstrated that views were mixed, and some investigators found it was more comfortable for them to interview by telephone and remain unseen to the subject of the investigation. Moreover, a further mapping of these findings to the coding for individual vs group experiences found that the latter preference for telephone interviewing was heavily identified as an individual preference and not seen as advantageous to the team as a whole.

I have used interview data for the examples here, but observation data can be similarly coded according to a Framework Analysis. However, as with the responses to a questionnaire (see above), it might be that these data are already grouped according to a framework created by the collection mechanism. In the observations of the RRT/MRT hearings, my data were already coded according to 'question type' (see above) and a range of other specific phenomena that I was interested in such as 'Engage and Explain utterances.' This latter coding is related to those phrases or discourse sequences used by Members to build rapport ('Engage') and describe the nature of the hearing ('Explain'). Like the 'question types' coding, the literature on best practice investigative interviewing lists specific features of the Engage and Explain phase that I sought to identify in the hearings. One example of this would be a clear instruction to the Applicant about how to answer questions such as 'tell me everything, even the little things that you think are not important.' Research shows that instructing interviewees in this way will increase the reliability and quantity of their responses (Geiselman, Fisher, MacKinnon, & Holland, 1986). When it came to coding the data from the observations, I listed the types of Engage and Explain utterances that Members used under a relevant heading, and I created a similar list of the question types and various other phenomena that I had been observing during the hearings. I used the brief notes made during the hearings as my data for this coding exercise.

Coding and analysing the data from the questionnaires from the RCB project was made very straightforward by the use of software (Qualtrics) which enabled reports of the responses. I used these reports to identify areas of weakness or strength in the team's knowledge and patterns of commonality or difference in their attitudes to various interviewing techniques. These findings could be cross-referenced with the interview data, and used directly to inform the content of the training package.

We will return to the interpretation of the data and show how these findings can be triangulated with other data sets in the next section, but before that, we will briefly discuss the analysis of the third data source, *Training materials*. As written texts, the analytical approach to these data will be similar to that used for the legislation and regulatory texts. Researchers might find that there are limited materials to analyse in this data set. Sometimes prior training courses are subject to commercial in-confidence restrictions, but mostly, the reason will simply be that there has not been any dedicated training material developed for the team or unit. Exceptions to this are police departments and other law enforcement agencies. While there is a practical and professional benefit to having a deep knowledge of how the team has been trained to interview in the past, there is also an important contribution that this data source can make to the project: by comparing the content of the prior training with the observation and interview data, it is possible to see what has been retained and what is regarded as important or useful by the team members themselves. It is also possible to identify gaps between 'known unknowns' and 'unknown unknowns.' A comparison between the two projects described here provides an example of what I mean by this: investigators from the RCB were almost universally modest in their assessment of their knowledge about interviewing theory, while Members from the RRT with a law qualification tended to be confident that years of legal practice had provided ample knowledge of 'good interviewing.' An examination of the training materials used by each group showed that in fact the RCB investigators had at least been exposed to cognitive interviewing theory, whereas the RRT Members had never been provided with any training in Cognitive Interviewing theory and there was no evidence that they were even aware of the existence of theories of interviewing. By following up these findings with a questionnaire (for the RCB team) and further discussions with senior staff (in the RRT unit), I was able to confirm that for the RCB team, the concepts of CI theory were known unknowns – they knew it existed but they could not recall the details – whereas for the RRT Members, CI was an unknown unknown – they had never heard of it and they were unaware that they lacked this important area of knowledge.

Interpreting data

Bringing together the findings of the three main areas of data analysis provided a rich description of the practical and intellectual challenges for developing appropriate interviewing training materials in the two projects.

RCB

Investigators in the RCB had powers to question witnesses in order to investigate alleged breaches of the law regulating the financial and administrative governance of specific organisations. Many of their cases involved alleged fraud or misuse of funds by staff in these organisations and RCBs investigations were generally very long-running and usually involved book-keeping irregularities occurring over many years. The witnesses to the alleged offending were often close colleagues of the suspect and not inclined to cooperate with the RCB. Investigations were conducted using the telephone or video conferencing, as mentioned earlier, and the investigators themselves were primarily from a financial, accounting or legal background, rather than law enforcement. In other words, the environment was most unlike a typical police investigation.

120 *Legal process*

The analysis found that there are systematic differences between interviews conducted by investigators in the RCB and police interviewing. These differences relate to, among other things:

- the legislative framework (and especially the decision to compel a witness to be interviewed),
- the staff backgrounds and expertise,
- the attitude of interviewees,
- the perception of the Branch amongst the regulated organisations, and
- the specific use of evidence in cases.

The data also revealed that the nature of the offences was substantially different from most police investigations, in that offences investigated by the RCB tended to relate to often mundane administrative activities occurring repeatedly over a number of months or even years, rather than a single incident usually occurring in the recent past. This has a considerable impact on the use of cognitive techniques for enhancing memory recall, which have primarily been designed for police investigations of a single, recent incident.

The method of interviewing was also substantially different from police interviewing due to the prevalence of telephone and video conference interviews, rather than the traditional face-to-face model used in policing. The rapport building strategies in these cases needed to be developed specifically for this remote interviewing environment.

People interviewed by the RCB were invariably connected in a dense network of workplace relationships involving complex loyalties and allegiances, which affected their willingness to provide information, even when they were not accused of wrongdoing themselves. This specific circumstance of RCB investigations also led to the presence of an organisational representative (usually a legal practitioner) in the interviews, as a 'support person' for the interviewee. This has an important impact on the capacity of the interviewers to conduct their interview without undue influence from a third party, especially when interruptions can threaten the integrity of the interviewee's memory recall process. The exact status of that person, with respect to their capacity or authority to provide legal advice to the interviewee, was identified as requiring further clarification by the RCB.

The extent of differences between RCB investigations and police investigations means that most advanced interviewing training programs would be unsuitable for RCB investigators because they are based on the police investigative model. The best approach to RCB interviewing training was to draw on the research that underpins such advanced interviewing techniques to develop an adapted model of interviewing specifically for the RCB environment. This was greatly assisted by the fact that staff had a working knowledge of cognitive interviewing principles and techniques, although they were not confident in their deployment. This was most likely a result of the infrequency of interviews conducted by the branch and a need for regular practice interviews and a review process was identified by staff. This finding indicated that interview practice role plays would be an extremely important part of the learning experience. As a result, a substantial amount of time within the training course was dedicated to running a mock investigation that involved a cast of actors playing witnesses and suspects and, over several days, exposed the participants to different interviewing scenarios requiring specific strategies and skills learned in the course.

RRT

Rather than provide another broad summary of the project findings, this section presents an in-depth description of one of the findings in the RRT project. This is intended to demonstrate how the analysis of data drawn from multiple sources, as described in the previous section, can be interpreted within a linguistic theoretical framework in order to provide insights both to the client organisation and to the academic community.

In the RRT, it was observed that Members generally start the hearing with a 'preamble.' The 'preamble' to the hearing is a process of explanation to the Applicant and any other participants to explain how the hearing will proceed and the roles to be played by those present. This is partially scripted in order to comply with relevant laws, but there are specific features of an RRT hearing preamble that are open to the Member's interpretation, and can influence the subsequent interaction. As mentioned above, part of the coding framework that was applied during the observations was the specific phrases or discourse units that could be categorised as Engage and Explain utterances according the interviewing theories. This coding framework highlighted a very specific phenomenon: during the preamble, Members often referred to a large quantity of information at their disposal, and some would gesture towards a very tall stack of files on the bench. Usually they used a phrase such as 'I have read a lot about your case in your files.' Analysis of the interview data showed that individuals were concerned to convey to Applicants the sense that they did not have to re-tell their entire story to the Member, either because they didn't want to waste time (i.e. for organisational reasons) or because they wanted the Applicant to feel their story was important and acknowledged (i.e. for interpersonal reasons). However, when they did this in the hearing, Members did not make it clear to Applicants whether they had a detailed knowledge of the contents of the files, or merely a familiarity with the key points covered therein. For Applicants, the difference is crucial, and the confusion caused considerable discursive difficulties in the subsequent interactions.

Members were emphatic in the interviews that elicit relevant responses to questions and stopping the Applicant from repeating detailed stories already documented in the Departmental files was a significant obstacle to making an informed decision. They used examples from hearings to demonstrate the problems they encountered in trying to convey to the Applicants the importance of providing new information to support their case. They described Applicants either giving very short answers to questions, or giving partial answers that were of uncertain relevance. Time in the hearing is very limited, and much of it can be wasted, according to the Members, if Applicants were not able to answer the questions appropriately. It seemed a strange state of affairs that the Members were so keen to elicit details from Applicants, and the Applicants were equally keen to tell their story and support their case for asylum, and yet the gap between the information required and the information provided so often seemed to grow ever wider as the hearing progressed.

In order to understand the problem, it is useful to consider the feature of the RRT hearing preamble described earlier in relation to rules of conversational implicature derived through the study of pragmatics. The Gricean maxim of quantity (give as much information as needed, and no more) generally restricts what is allowable in conversation to new information because information that is already known to everyone present is usually regarded as extraneous (Grice, 1975). However, being unsure of how much information is known to the Member already, but being assured that *something* is known – perhaps everything in the case files – Applicants will find it almost impossible to know how much detail to provide in their responses to questions. As the hearing proceeds and the Member asks various questions about the case, it is very difficult for the Applicant to assess what the Member already knows. In other words, when the Applicant is unclear about what exactly the Member knows, it then becomes problematic for them to try to frame their response as 'new' information. The Applicant might provide a minimal amount of information to a question and wait for a request for more information. However, the Member cannot be too specific about what they are seeking to find out for fear of 'leading the witness' and undermining the validity of the Applicant's evidence. The result can be a frustrating exchange of roundabout questioning and vague responses in which both participants are trying to test the extent of the other's knowledge.

The research demonstrated that this problem might not stem from misdirected or misinterpreted questions, as seemed to be the case, but from an otherwise innocuous habit of the Members during the preamble. Simply by being more specific about the known file information, or telling Applicants to answer questions even if they thought the Member might already know the answer, the situation would be vastly improved. Reminding Applicants that they can ask questions or clarify a question from the Member and allowing time for Applicants to add to their responses are other strategies that could alleviate the problem.

Applications to legal practice and procedures

Consultancy research projects such as these usually result in very practical and applied outcomes for the clients. In the justice sector, we would reasonably anticipate that these outcomes will support fairer decision-making and improve access to justice for community members. Thus the application of this research to legal practice and procedures is somewhat straightforward.

The project for the RCB investigators resulted in a specialised training course and a set of recommendations for future improvements in their interviewing practices. With improved interviewing practices, the investigators are able to conduct higher quality investigations and deliver more robust evidence to the

Commission. Individual officers also reported feeling more confident in their role and better equipped to manage difficult situations. As a unit, the RCB now had an evidence base for their interviewing practices which could support them in case of a review of their information gathering procedure.

Training was also delivered to the RRT/MRT Members who reported that the insights such as the use of specific types of question and strategies for the Engage and Explain phase were particularly helpful for their practice. As in the RCB, the opportunity to draw on an evidence-based set of interviewing techniques was cited as an important step towards making their hearings less vulnerable to claims of unfair treatment in an appeal or other review process.

Within both of the projects, there were also more specific ways in which linguistic research contributed to legal practices and procedures.

In the RCB, the problem of receipt markers in remote interviewing (telephone or video conferencing) was addressed through participatory action research. Investigators were taught the theory of minimal responses, including receipt markers and continuers as well as other discourse markers (e.g. change of frame). They were then able to listen to recordings of their own interviews and observe the speech behaviour of their colleagues and identify the most suitable and neutral receipt marker to use in their remote interviews.

In the RRT, the application of the Gricean maxim of quantity to the way in which Members handled the preamble is an example of a highly specific and technical piece of knowledge about how language works that can have dramatic implications in a tribunal hearing. In a review tribunal there is not the opportunity to review every aspect of the case, or to start again with an entirely fresh narrative from the Applicant. The cases rely on the Applicant to provide additional evidence to support their claim in relation to specific points that the Department of Immigration has found unsatisfactory. Therefore, their capacity to provide additional evidence to that already before the Member means they must successfully navigate the known and unknown information, and all this is usually mediated through an interpreter as well. By conducting research that takes account of the relevant legislation regulating the review tribunal, the attitudes and beliefs of Members, the actual practices of Members in the hearing and the relevant linguistic framework, forensic linguists can contribute directly to the improvement of the justice system.

Final word

To the extent that professional development training delivery forms a regular part of our work as academics in such an applied field, it is important that we maintain high standards of research-based teaching. Professional staff in the justice and law enforcement sectors work in a challenging and dynamic environment, often subject to the whims of political forces and community sentiment. When working with these organisations, I try to separate the core skills of the job from the shifting sands of professional development fads. I find it interesting that while most of these organisations have interviewing or information elicitation at the heart of their operations, many have not considered that linguistic insights into questioning might be beneficial. Instead, I have seen organisations arrange professional development seminars with experts in fields that are either peripheral to their core business, or unsupported by scientific research. A good example of this was the engagement of a 'human lie detector' by the Royal Australian College of General Practitioners to speak at their annual conference in 2017 and teach doctors how to identify malingerers.[3] As discussed in Chapter 4 of this book, lie detection has almost no scientific basis, and yet it was considered a more suitable skill for medical practitioners than scientifically rigorous interviewing methods. There are those in our field who dismiss professional development training as a waste of their time, usually because they feel they are having little impact on practices. However, I would remind such colleagues that if we refuse these opportunities to engage, we risk leaving professional development for justice workers in the hands of underqualified presenters using unscientific methods. Moreover, as this chapter has demonstrated, not only can we engage positively with professional justice workers, but we can learn from their experiences and undertake enriching research projects that contribute to their training as well as to the field of linguistic knowledge.

Notes

1 In Australia, hearings in the Migration Review Tribunal and the Refugee Review Tribunal are conducted by the same pool of Members. This is in part because cases can move from one Tribunal to another, such as when a student visa decision is reviewed by the MRT, the visa is granted and the recipient subsequently applies for asylum once they have arrived in Australia to study. Their case might then be reviewed by the RRT, if the Department decides not to grant the protection visa. As a result of this, MRT decisions are sometimes made with a view to the likelihood of the Applicant subsequently applying for asylum in Australia.
2 Examples include Atlas ti 6.0 (www.atlasti.com), HyperRESEARCH 2.8 (www.researchware.com), Max QDA (www.maxqda.com), The Ethnograph 5.08QSR N6 (www.qsrinternational.com), QSR Nvivo (www.qsrinternational.com). Weft QDA (www.pressure.to/qda), Open code 3.4 (www8.umu.se).
3 https://www.smh.com.au/healthcare/racgp-uses-human-lie-detector-to-help-gps-sniff-out-deception-among-patients-20171026-gz8v1t.html

References

Dando, C., Wilcock, R., & Milne, R. (2008). The cognitive interview: Inexperienced police officers' perceptions of their witness/victim interviewing practices. *Legal and Criminological Psychology, 13*(1), 59–70.

Geiselman, R. E., Fisher, R. P., MacKinnon, D. P., & Holland, H. L. (1986). Enhancement of eyewitness memory with the cognitive interview. *American Journal of Psychology, 99*, 385–401.

Grice, H. P. (1975). Logic and conversation. In P. Cole & J. L. Morgan (Eds.), *Speech acts (Syntax and semantics volume III)* (pp. 41–58). New York: Academic Press.

Labov, W. (2006). *The social stratification of English in New York city*. Cambridge, UK: Cambridge University Press.

Minichiello, V., Aroni, R., & Hays, T. (2008). *In-depth interviewing: Principles, techniques, analysis*. Frenchs Forest, NSW: Pearson Education Australia.

Mitchell, M. S., & Koen Jr, C. M. (2012). Guidelines for conducting bulletproof workplace investigations: Part I—preparation and interviewing issues. *The Health Care Manager, 31*(2), 105–111.

Parlett, M., & Hamilton, D. (1972). Evaluation as illumination: A new approach to the study of innovatory programs. Occasional Paper.

Stake, R. E. (1995). *The art of case study research*. Thousand Oaks: Sage Publications.

8 Access to justice
Post-colonial language attitudes

> In July 2013, I was attending the Biennial Conference of the International Association for Forensic Linguists in Mexico City when I had an encounter that made worthwhile all the long-haul flights, epic queues for passport control and even the dose of Montezuma's Revenge I suffered on the flight back to Europe for my next conference: I met Mozambique's first forensic linguist, Dr Eliseu Mabasso from the Universidade Eduardo Mondlane (UEM), Maputo. Dr Mabasso had just given a paper on police interviewing in Mozambique, demonstrating the considerable barrier to justice suffered by those Mozambicans who did not speak adequately fluent Portuguese to navigate the complexities of the legal process (Mabasso, 2013; Mabasso & Heydon, forthcoming). One of the aspects of Mabasso's work that most interested me was the clear influence of justice processes that had nothing to do with the civil law system inherited from the Portuguese colonial power. In the police interview excerpts that Mabasso presented, there were interactions that were instead drawing on the customary or traditional law procedures such as the mediation between the suspect and the victim by the police officer. This was most evident in the domestic violence (DV) cases that Mabasso presented in his paper. I was immediately fascinated by the complexity of the problem and having recently begun collaborative work with colleagues specialising in the prevention of violence against women (Heydon & Powell, 2018), I was interested to see whether some of these issues might be arising amongst women experiencing DV in Melbourne's migrant communities. Following the conference, Mabasso and I stayed in touch and when the opportunity arose in March 2014, I visited him in Maputo and we began work on a slowly evolving research collaboration investigating the interaction of legal pluralism and language policy in DV reporting and prosecution in Maputo. This chapter presents our approach to the project and draws on published work (Heydon & Mabasso, 2018) as well as unpublished industry reports resulting from extensive field interviews in 2016.

Introduction

Language policy in post-colonial states is a complex area of governance that can greatly influence justice outcomes. By applying our knowledge of language as a social, cultural and political force, linguists make an important contribution to policymaking in the justice sector. However, policy-related research is not as common in linguistics research training as it is in fields such as criminology and law. Although a considerable quantity of literature regarding the most contested areas of language policy, such as the introduction of 11 official languages in the Republic of South Africa, has been undertaken by linguists working in those regions, in other countries there is less interest in such topics. In Mozambique, where the research presented in this chapter took place, the linguistics department in the main state university, UEM, focuses almost exclusively on core linguistics (in Portuguese, the official language) and language typology and documentation (of African languages). Yet, the language problem (Kamwangamalu & Kamwangamalu, 2016) remains a critical barrier to justice for many Mozambicans. This chapter will demonstrate how research into language policy can also encompass the investigation of practical linguistic issues that linguists are well-placed to address. The mechanism for this multifaceted approach is field interviews with stakeholders – a tool typically associated with policy research, but which can be used to identify very specific linguistic issues, as was the case with the research reported here.

The research presented in this chapter investigates the way that justice and social support agencies receive and process reports of abuse from victims of DV in Maputo. Although initially the focus of the research collaboration was on police interviewing, the research team has since broadened its enquiry to include the diverse ways in which DV cases might be reported by victims in Maputo. The team has also investigated the beliefs and assumptions that victims and others hold about DV in light of the customary law practices that are common in Mozambique. An important focus of the project was the use of languages other than Portuguese by victims during the reporting process, and in courtroom or other legal procedures.

Approach to the problem

Through the first field trip to Mozambique in 2014 and subsequent desktop research, the research team familiarised themselves with the legal, social and political context within which the research takes place.

Legal systems in Mozambique

The current government in Mozambique has its roots in the war of independence against Portuguese colonial rule, which ended when the country achieved independence from Portugal in 1975. The subsequent civil war, which lasted from 1976 to 1992, had a devastating impact on the Mozambican people and has left the country with high levels of poverty, poor infrastructure and a poorly resourced government. Mozambique's legal system can best be described as official legal pluralism, with formal recognition of customary law, a constitution and a written civil law code based on the colonial Portuguese legal regime, all of which operate within a socialist framework (Pimentel, 2011).

An important factor relevant to the present study is the impact of language on access to justice in each of the different legal systems. Whereas the institutions of the formal legal system (police and prosecutors, for instance) will conduct their inquiries in the official language – Portuguese – local community leaders or community police representatives can usually conduct their interactions with the victim and her family in a local Mozambican language. This issue is explored in more detail below.

Domestic violence in Mozambique

The 2012 Demographic and Health Survey (DHS) reported that one in three Mozambican women had experienced violence at least once since the age of 15. The same study found that '12% of women reported being forced to have sex at some point in their lifetime' (Instituto Nacional de Estatística, Ministerio da Saude, & MEASURE DHS/ICF International, 2012, p. 245). In 59% of these cases of sexual assault, the women did not seek any assistance or report the sexual violence to anyone (p. 273).

In 1998 a coalition came together for the All Against Violence campaign, which involved direct support for victims, public education and counselling, training and education on human rights and gender inequalities, and research on violence against women (Loforte, 2009). This placed pressure on the government to act and comply with the United Nations' Convention on the Elimination of All Forms of Discrimination Against Women (CEDAW) and specifically the Optional Protocol to CEDAW, which was ratified by Mozambique in 2008 (Loforte, 2009).

In 2009, following these campaigns and the ratification of CEDAW, the Mozambican parliament passed a specific DV law, which prohibits physical, financial, emotional and sexual violence against women, including marital rape.[1] In 2012, the Mozambican government implemented a national plan to address violence against women across five provinces. This included a television and radio campaign led by the Ministry of Women that informed women of their rights under the legislation (OECD Development Centre, 2018).

Language policy in Mozambique

As set out in article 10 of the 2004 Constitution (see Appendix A), Portuguese is Mozambique's official language, and is therefore the language of the legal system. However, according to official statistics only 40% of the population are at least partly fluent in Portuguese, and in rural populations, the level of Portuguese proficiency drops to 25% (Mabasso, 2013). Only 7% of the population considered

Portuguese their mother tongue and the vast majority of Mozambicans have as their native language one of several Bantu languages.

Article 98 of the Criminal Procedure Code requires courts to appoint an interpreter for non-Portuguese speaking defendants. While some attempt is made by courts to provide interpreters, there are few professionally trained interpreters available and very often, courts will use a bilingual member of staff, or even a member of the community instead of a trained interpreter.

For victims of DV, the language barrier is likely to be even greater than for the general population. For 93% of the population Portuguese is a second language. It is acquired through education, and maintained though ongoing workplace engagement. Given that a great many women experiencing DV are living below the poverty line, are not in paid work and have only a primary school education, they are less likely than the general population to speak Portuguese with sufficient fluency to conduct legal negotiations or provide a detailed and accurate account of their experiences.

Identifying research questions

Within the political, cultural and legal environment described above, it appears that *language* is indeed an inhibiting factor in women's capacity to access justice following an experience of DV. Thus, language policy and practices are important aspects of DV reporting that require further examination and explication. Given that this is the first study to address the language-based iniquities of the Mozambican justice system that routinely disadvantage women reporting DV, we first sought to ascertain how legal professionals and social support workers understand the language challenges for non-Portuguese speakers reporting DV in Mozambique. The research questions that guided our interview protocol and analysis were as follows:

1 What are the stakeholders' perceptions of linguistic diversity and Portuguese proficiency amongst their clientele?[2]
2 What are the strategies used by stakeholders to respond to the linguistic diversity and level of Portuguese proficiency amongst their clientele; and
3 What are the resources stakeholders have available to them to disseminate information to their clientele and the public at large.

Data collection

In order to respond to the research questions, qualitative semi-structured interviews were conducted with key stakeholders in ten government and non-government organisations in the DV and justice sectors (see below). Over a period of two weeks in March 2016, the research team visited justice and social support organisations which were selected in part on the basis of an earlier field study in 2014, and in part through suggestions from existing participants (i.e. snowballing).

130 *Legal process*

The team conducted interviews with staff across a range of roles, from frontline legal advisors and counsellors, to directors and senior government officials.

Interviews were conducted by an English-speaking interviewer (Heydon) with the assistance of a Portuguese-English professional interpreter. A second researcher fluent in Portuguese and English (Mabasso) provided a supporting commentary on aspects of the participants' contributions, clarifying cultural or political points and assisting the professional interpreter with technical terms as required. Interviews were recorded electronically whenever possible and the researchers took extensive field notes to support the analysis of data.

Interview schedules (see Heydon & Mabasso, 2018) were devised for the interviews with staff in different agencies in order to support our research goals. The interview questions sought to elucidate the intersection of customary law and language diversity in the reporting of DV by women in Maputo. An important supporting theme in our interviews was therefore the role of language in facilitating or restricting access to justice for women reporting DV.

Four official government justice agencies participated in the study: the Prosecutor-General's Department (PGR), the Judicial Training College, the Special Police Unit for Gabinetes de Atendimento a Mulher e Criança Vitimas de Violencia Doméstica ('Offices to Assist Women and Child Victims of Domestic Violence') and Academia de Ciências Policiais, the police training college.[3]

Four civil society organisations that provide legal advice and counselling services to women in Maputo also participated in the study: MULEIDE, Associação Moçambicana das Mulheres de Carreira Jurídica (AMMCJ), Liga Mocambicana dos Direitos Humanos (the Liga) and Forum Mulher (FM).

Two further organisations were represented in the research. One was the network of community police officers and the other was the UEM Centre for Human Rights. The UEM Centre for Human Rights was primarily a training organisation, providing professional development in human rights issues for (mainly) government employees. The community police unit is essentially a local security and dispute resolution agency sitting at the intersection of the formal civil law system and the customary law system. Its role in responding to DV cases was especially important from a linguistic perspective and will be discussed in more detail below.

As in the study of interviewing in a regulatory compliance agency (see Chapter 7), data from the Mozambican interviews were analysed simultaneously in the course of the interview and inductively through subsequent transcription and coding based on emerging themes (Minichiello, Aroni, & Hays, 2008). Due to the presence of an interpreter mediating the communication, it became easier to conduct simultaneous analysis and pursue themes as they emerged than is usually the case in a monolingual interview. As a result, the interviews tended to be exploratory and each interview covered a more diverse range of topics than those indicated in the original question schedule. The findings were therefore of two main kinds: there were findings from the data generated in response to the question schedule that were broadly comparable across the entire data set and then there were findings that were more specific to an agency and related to its function in the justice system. In order to identify suitable recommendations for stakeholder organisations, the generalised findings were most useful. However, for each participating organisation, the research team also prepared an individual report that included a summary of the findings specific to that organisation.

Data analysis

To demonstrate the range of findings that emerged from the interviews, this section presents the analysis of interview data collected from three representative organisations in the study: the Judicial Training College representing formal government agencies; FM representing non-government organisations; and the community police unit representing the integration of customary law in the justice system. Findings from these three organisations are presented below and in the case of the first two, each set of findings is set out to reflect the three research questions: perceptions of linguistic diversity; responses to linguistic diversity; and resources for communicating with the public. The third interview followed a somewhat different trajectory because the role of a community police officer (or community leader) is frontline response rather than policymaking. Thus in this interview, we gained considerable insight into the day-to-day operations of mediating disputes relating to DV, but less information about organisational responses to linguistic diversity.

Judicial Training College

The Judicial Training College plays an important role in training judicial officers who will investigate crimes under the inquisitorial model in their courts. The Judicial Training College was our main point of contact with the judiciary in this research, and an important source of information about practices and attitudes of judicial officers in Maputo. State judges generally preside over cases with two community judges, whose function and background loosely resemble those of jurors in an adversarial courtroom.

Data from the interview with the Director of the Judicial Training College indicated that language diversity was an issue that strained the resources of the courts. The Director pointed out that current law requires magistrates to use Portuguese at all stages of the court process; however, if any of the witnesses are non-Portuguese speakers then the law states that an interpreter should be hired. Therefore, the court first determines if a person speaks Portuguese so that they can hire an interpreter for the trial if required. This suggests that it is left to court officials to decide the person's competency in Portuguese. The Director went on to explain that if the trial process starts and one person does not speak Portuguese the trial is delayed to find an interpreter. However, it was clear that interpreters were by no means readily available and the Director noted that due to increasing linguistic diversity a permanent interpreter service for immediate use is needed. Under the present arrangement the state pays the cost for casual interpreters.

Another area where linguistic diversity impacts on the judiciary is in the quality of evidence in witness statements. The Director noted the importance of investigation evidence to judicial decision-making in court. She observed that there are some obstacles to collecting reliable evidence and that at times, analysing the evidence is difficult and people are wrongly condemned. In her experience, these difficulties could be related to fundamental questions that should be asked in an investigation (when, where, how etc.), which suggests that such basic information is sometimes missing from evidential accounts.

The Director noted several areas of weakness within the current system, including that the present court interpreter service does not cover all the languages spoken by people presenting in court, that even highly competent interpreters find it difficult to learn the legal terminology and find equivalent terms in local languages, and that because the interpreters are not always readily available, judges will proceed without them in order to save time. Sometimes, legal officials working in the court are used as ad hoc interpreters in the absence of a trained interpreter, and sometimes judicial officers stop the court interpreter to correct their translation of specific terms.

It was clear from the Director's responses that the court officials are accustomed to working around the shortcomings of the present language services in order to manage linguistic diversity amongst the witnesses.

Some of the ways that would improve language services included the use of plain Portuguese to explain legal terms. The Director explained that since the judicial officer must use Portuguese in court, the use of plain Portuguese legal terms would facilitate understanding by interpreters and ensure the interpretation is accurate. She noted that during the trial it might be necessary to explain things in simple terms even if in their own notes judicial officers will use the formal legal terms. She commented that they 'need to train our magistrates to ask questions in a very simple way so people can understand.'

The Director's view was that producing a dictionary of plain Portuguese legal terms would be useful but stakeholders, including the judiciary, lawyers and police, would need training to know how to use it. She suggested that the Judicial College might raise awareness of the use of the tool and involve judicial officers to provide technical training on how to use the dictionary. This indicates the pivotal role of the College in disseminating information and communicating changes to stakeholders in the justice system. The Director also suggested that the College can provide assistance in writing the dictionary and in conducting interviews with stakeholders in the justice field to inform the structure and content of the dictionary.

Forum Mulher

FM is a network of 88 organisations and institutions for women's rights that operate at the provincial level. Formed in the mid-1990s, FM conducts programs with a special focus on local organisations, but all actions are part of the network activities. Language diversity and access to justice are key concerns of FM. These issues are connected to the different pathways that women take and the entry points to the criminal justice system. If a woman is in a more remote area or otherwise isolated, and she is seeking assistance at the community level, she will approach the community leader (or Community Policing Unit – see below) and this might lead to her seeking assistance from customary courts. However, in district and provincial centres, women have access to civil societies who assist victims in their cases (for instance MULEIDE, and AMMCJ, who were included in this study). The health system and hospitals provide a third avenue for assistance, and finally, there are now the 'gabinetes' (the Special Police Unit for DV, also included in this study), and health-based multidisciplinary centres. Notably, the interviewee did not mention the direct approach that a victim can make to a prosecutor at an office of the PGR (Heydon & Mabasso, 2018, p. 91).

Each of these pathways presents different language or cultural challenges. For instance, a major concern about community leaders or community police is that, without adequate education about DV, these men might in fact be re-victimising women seeking their assistance by adopting customary principles based on traditional gender roles. Since DV was classified as a crime in 2009, community leaders and community police are not supposed to deal with such cases, and must pass them onto the formal justice system, either to the police or the PGR. However, because of their local knowledge and connection to the communities, and because the courts are more distant and potentially inaccessible, many community leaders still believe that it is appropriate for them to deal with DV cases. On a more positive note, the interview data find that community leaders can play an important role in producing evidence for the courts, where a case has been transferred to the prosecutor's office. This is especially important to our study, because community leaders and community police tend to use the local language of the women rather than Portuguese.

For those women who approach civil society organisations like FM, they will be assisted by activists, paralegals and lawyers who receive training in language and cultural issues. FM recognises that knowledge of local languages is required by their staff, and that outside of Maputo especially, most women do not have sufficient Portuguese proficiency to be understood or to navigate the legal system. The officers of the civil society organisations provide assistance with the Portuguese legal terminology for their clients, and for those cases that go to court, language assistance is provided by paralegals and lawyers. Although civil society organisations are outside the formal legal system, they are still able to play an important role in providing legal assistance in court, and this can include language assistance. However, given the limited resources and operational capacity of the FM, legal staff do not always speak the local language of their client, and this can create difficulties in court.

According to the FM interview data, language assistance in the courtroom is often provided by the elected judges, who are community members, and, like a jury, are restricted to judging the facts of the case. These community judges usually speak local languages, and play a prominent role as ad hoc interpreters, explaining the proceedings to non-Portuguese speaking victims. However, as they lack legal training, they do not themselves always understand the legal aspects of the case, or the legal terminology. The view of the FM is that in order to help victims in court, everyone concerned needs to understand human rights, at the very least. But the lack of language training and specialist training in legal terminology is clearly a considerable challenge for all parties.

To respond to these challenges, the interview data suggest that FM staff focus mainly on advocacy, but they also engage in capacity building and training programs. Many of the education programs are intended to raise awareness of women's rights and FM produces booklets, videos and plays that explain legal rights to Mozambicans. They have produced explanation booklets that include cartoons in local languages and simplified information. Education programs, including international human rights education tools, are disseminated through these publications, seminars and training. FM takes seriously its international obligations to fight discrimination.

One strategy is through the community leaders themselves, and there is a very high priority on capacity building amongst community leaders, given that they live in the victim's community and the formal justice agencies are distant and inaccessible. The main focus is on educating community leaders about the limitations of their role in DV cases, how to forward cases to the PGR (public prosecutions office) or police and how to collect evidence appropriately and avoid victim-blaming.

A training video in Portuguese was produced by FM to explain to both victims and police the correct procedure for investigating DV cases, how the police are to be involved in the case and what constitutes good and bad practice. However, it was unclear how this video was being used in practice.

The interview data indicate that FM is already in a good position to produce and disseminate any educational materials that are produced, but there seems to be a gap in local language materials. Additionally, there is a skills gap in the courts: legal professionals, including judges, lawyers and paralegals, have the required legal knowledge but tend not to speak local languages; on the other hand, community judges or jurors usually have knowledge of the local language spoken by the victim, but have no legal training. To some extent, civil society agencies are able to fill this gap by providing their legal staff with language training, but it appears that this is a very limited resource, and in any case, as these staff are not professional interpreters, they are not trained or educated in translating complex legal terminology to a local African language, or even in simplifying legal concepts using Portuguese.

Community police unit

The community police unit represents a bridge between government and non-government agencies, and was established to mediate the relationship between citizens and the formal justice system. Language diversity is one of the factors that influences a citizen's decision to take their case to the local community police officers rather than make a formal report. Whereas the institutions of the formal legal system (police and prosecutors, for instance) will conduct their inquiries in the official language – Portuguese – local community leaders or community police representatives can usually conduct their interactions with the victim and her family in a local Mozambican language.

In rural areas where police presence is limited, these officers assume the role of community leaders and have specific powers to investigate complaints, within clearly articulated (though not always observed) limits.[4] With the criminalisation of DV in 2009, this changed their role in marital disputes, especially. Whereas it was accepted practice for community police officers to mediate DV disputes and usually counsel the couple to cease fighting and live together peaceably, now they are required to pass on a report of such cases to police or the PGR.

It became clear in our fieldwork, however, that it was not uncommon for community police officers to assess the DV incident as 'non-violent' or non-criminal in order to avoid sending the case on to the courts. They saw this as providing a service to their community and saving people the expense of a trial, which is no doubt a legitimate concern. There was also a strong view that marriages were to be preserved, as they provide the only source of financial support for most women and their children. Again, this is undoubtedly true, although legally women are entitled to receive maintenance payments from their ex-husbands.

Interpreting the data

One of the most important themes to emerge from the data as a whole was the limitations that language placed on the options available to women reporting DV. For those women who had low proficiency in Portuguese, their most accessible option was to report to a community police officer or block leader using their local language. However, while the community police might have been able to offer a linguistically compatible option, our research revealed grave concerns that women reporting via this avenue would not have their case raised with the relevant authority and were likely to be encouraged to return to their husband where they faced continuing violence.

Moreover, the data analysis found that there were limited educational resources for non-Portuguese speaking women that might have informed them of their human and civil rights. Thus these women were less likely to pursue a legal option that might have enforced property laws and ensured that their abusive partners would not entrap them in a violent marriage through financial means. On the other hand, there was recognition that in situations of extreme poverty, formal legal proceedings were beyond the financial reach of families experiencing a DV crisis. Many respondents acknowledged that in such situations, perpetrators as well as victims could gain a greater practical benefit from the intervention of a community police officer, especially given the 'rule-of-law deficiency' in Mozambique (Pimentel, 2011).

This finding reinforces the importance of contextualising research into DV reporting and linguistic diversity within the limitations of the justice system in Mozambique. The Open Society Initiative report on the rule of law in Mozambique describes the situation as follows:

> On balance, despite its reform efforts, the state is unable to guarantee access to justice for its citizens, particularly those living in remote areas. The reality

for most Mozambicans is that the judicial courts are inaccessible, blocked by a range of obstacles including financial constraints and their physical location. As a result, many citizens continue to rely on alternative mechanisms of dispute resolution, including community courts and traditional or other local leaders.

(Open Society Initiative for Southern Africa, 2006, p. 121)

In a study of violence against women that surveyed both police and community respondents, Saini, Cumbe, and Levy (2013) found that a lack of transparency in the legal process is a factor that discourages the reporting of sexual assault. This was exemplified by respondents who cited a tendency of the courts to transmute prison terms into fines, and the high level of influence that wealth or social status could have in court outcomes. Added to this, the study found that girls were fearful of the stigma and discrimination attached to reporting sexual assault which could ruin their marriage prospects (Saini et al., 2013). One report suggests that women who make a formal complaint face hostility from the relatives of their husband or partner, which can be translated into threats and physical aggression, isolation or denial of access to resources (Arthur & Mejia, 2007). There is often a rise in violence by the aggressor subsequent to police intervention (Arthur & Mejia, 2007).

Although this context of corruption and stigma is powerful disincentives for women reporting DV, these barriers will endure for longer if women are unable to understand or communicate in the language of the justice system. Providing a range of resources for women in local languages will better support victim-survivors when they do approach a more progressive agency such as the special DV police units or advocacy NGOs like FM.

Perhaps the most important contribution that the research team were able to make to this area was the identification of the specific linguistic issues that prevented the accommodation of multilingual participants in the justice system. The research found that a key difficulty for all participants and stakeholders trying to provide better local language services was the incompatibility of indigenous African languages with the formal Portuguese legal words and phrases. In many of our interviews, participants described the difficulty of finding appropriate words and phrases in Bantu languages to convey the precise legal meaning of Portuguese legal terminology. This is not a problem that can be overcome with more and better-trained interpreters, although interpreter services certainly need more funding in Mozambique. It is a problem that requires applied linguistic knowledge combined with legal expertise. However, this problem is not unique and linguists in Australia have been working to address the same issue that arises between Aboriginal languages and formal legal English terms. The Australian response has been a Plain English Legal Dictionary (Aboriginal Resource and Development Services, 2015) which provides definitions of legal terms in non-technical, simple English phrases supplemented by pictures and stories for context. For interpreters, this resource can be used as a front translation, providing agreed definitions using vocabulary and syntax that is suitable for rendering into an Aboriginal language with no loss or distortion of the legal meaning.

A research study that only considered the problem of linguistic diversity from a public policy or human rights perspective might not have identified the technical difficulty of semantic equivalence across languages in Africa. Those studies might well have identified solutions such as more funding for interpreters and African-language human rights information. But a study by linguists has the capacity to engage at the level of the language ecology. Crucially, in this case, we were able to observe the structural incompatibility between a modern colonial language like Portuguese that has evolved to accommodate a complete range of registers and domains, and Bantu languages whose development of formal and technical vocabularies has been stifled by post-colonial enforcement of Portuguese monolingualism. Importantly, academic knowledge sharing and cross-disciplinary collaboration can provide a potential solution to this problem in the form of a plain Portuguese legal dictionary.

Final word

While there is some potential for this research to effect positive change in Maputo, there is no escaping the size or scope of the problem of violence against women in Mozambique. Progress on the project has been slow and at the time of writing, resources to develop the dictionary have yet to be found. Of course, it would be naïve of any researcher to believe that a few field interviews and research reports will do much to help women to achieve equal rights and freedom from oppression. However, a hidden value of field work for us as academics is the opportunity to meet and listen to people telling their story in their local setting. While it might be difficult to judge the value of our research from the comforts of our university work-stations, I had no difficulty finding the motivation to continue the project, however slow our progress, whilst sitting on a garden wall with women waiting for legal help at MULEIDE, or waiting in the foyer of the Special Police Unit while the Chief interviewed a woman with visible bruises and a black eye, and a girl barely out of her teens made a complaint at the counter, surrounded by her sisters and cousins. Many times in the course of the field research in Maputo, I interviewed professional women whose lives had been shaped by the very patriarchal domination that they now seek to resist and subvert for the benefit of all Mozambicans. In the face of such courage and determination, how can I not choose to persevere?

Notes

1 Law on Domestic Violence Perpetrated Against Women Act, enacted 29 September 2009.
2 We use the term 'clientele' to refer to actual users of a DV service such as victim-survivors, suspects, relatives and friends of the same, and also potential users in the general public.
3 Understanding the context of the participants' work was an important aspect of the interviews; however it is beyond the scope of this chapter to detail each organisation's structure and function. See Heydon and Mabasso (2018) for more information.

4 The term 'leader' is also used to refer to a less formal role played by community authorities in urban areas. In our research, the interviewees consistently emphasised the importance of engaging with all of these authority figures, whether they were regarded as community leaders, block leaders or community police officers.

References

Aboriginal Resource and Development Services. (2015). *The Plain English Legal Dictionary*. Retrieved from https://ards.com.au/resources/downloadable/legal-dictionary-plain-english-to-djambarrpuyngu/

Arthur, M. J., & Mejia, M. (2007). *Rebuilding lives: The strategies of women survivors of domestic violence*. Maputo: WLSA Mozambique.

Heydon, G., & Mabasso, E. (2018). The impact of multilingualism on reporting domestic violence in Mozambique. *Language Matters, 49*(1), 84–106. doi:10.1080/10228195.2018.1444081

Heydon, G., & Powell, A. (2018). Written-response interview protocols: An innovative approach to confidential reporting and victim interviewing in sexual assault investigations. *Policing and Society, 28*(6), 631–646. doi:10.1080/10439463.2016.1187146

Instituto Nacional de Estatística, Ministerio da Saude, & MEASURE DHS/ICF International. (2012). *Moçambique, inquérito demográfico e de saúde 2011*. Maputo: Instituto Nacional de Estatistica.

Kamwangamalu, N. M., & Kamwangamalu, N. M. (2016). *Language policy and economics: The language question in Africa*. Houndsmill: Palgrave MacMillan UK.

Loforte, A. M. (2009). Social movements and violence against women in Mozambique: Landmarks on a journey. *Outras Vozes, 28* (November). Retrieved from Mulher e Lei na Africa Austral Moçambique website: http://www.wlsa.org.mz/article-social-movements-and-violence-against-women-in-mozambique-landmarks-on-a-journey/

Mabasso, E. (2013). *Official language, written and customary laws in Mozambican police stations*. Paper presented at the Paper presented to the 11th Biennial Conference of the Association of Forensic Linguists, Universidad Autonoma de Mexico.

Minichiello, V., Aroni, R., & Hays, T. (2008). *In-depth interviewing: Principles, techniques, analysis*. Frenchs Forest, Sydney: Pearson Education Australia.

OECD Development Centre. (2018). *Social institutions & gender index*. Retrieved from www.genderindex.org

Open Society Initiative for Southern Africa. (2006). *Mozambique: Justice sector and the rule of law*. Retrieved from http://www.unicef.org.mz/cpd/references/21-Mozambique Justice report (Eng).pdf

Pimentel, D. (2011). Legal pluralism in post-colonial Africa: Linking statutory and customary adjudication in Mozambique. *Yale Human Rights & Development Law Journal, 14*, 59.

Saini, F., Cumbe, E., & Levy, M. (2013). *Post-rape care for children in Mozambique: Assessment report*. Arlington, VA: USAID's AIDS Support and Technical Assistance Resources, AIDSTAR-One, Task Order 1.

9 Generating data for forensic linguistic research

Introduction

One of the first problems encountered by linguists embarking on a research career in forensic applications of language analysis is the difficulty of obtaining data. Subscribers to any of the regular newsletters or social media channels in the forensic linguistics field will be familiar with posts from students seeking advice about data sources for their proposed research study and as secretary of the International Association for Forensic Linguists (2011–2015), I received many such requests for assistance, especially about access to police interview data. Many of the approaches discussed in this volume use discourse analytic methods that require spoken language data such as original recordings of police interviews. Others, such as the forensic analyses of language evidence, use private correspondence or surveillance data obtained by police in the course of their investigations. These materials are unlikely to be available to student or early career researchers without considerable support from a research centre and strong connections to the sector. Yet it is vital to the advancement of the field that we extend our network of researchers both in number and in geographic reach. This means that forensic linguistic research needs to be accessible to those working and studying outside the existing research centres[1] and in regions where access to original data might be impractical or dangerous.[2]

While there has been considerable debate in the forensic psychology literature about the use of experimental methods (see below), less has been written about this in the forensic linguistic community (although see Hale & Napier (2013) for an overview of experimental methods in interpreter research). The discussion in the psychology journals has mainly been concerned with the cost to ecological validity posed by experimental methods that seek to maximise control over the variables and replicability of results. In the field of deception research in particular, there have been strong arguments against experimental methods on the grounds that the results are meaningless because they lack ecological validity (Armistead, 2011). As discussed in Chapter 4, proponents of lie detection methods are especially vocal in dismissing the extensive experimental research that finds that such lie detection methods are inaccurate or unreliable. The lie detection supporters argue that in a laboratory experiment, it is simply not possible to replicate the behavioural and linguistic responses that occur in the field due to the lack of real pressure on the subjects and the low consequences for them if they are not convincing. Chapter 4 provides an example of research that uses televised appeals for help in missing persons cases to analyse deceptive behaviour (where the person making the appeal is later proven to have been involved in the death or disappearance of the victim), but attaining ecological validity in experimental research involving police investigative methods remains problematic in forensic psychology.

In forensic linguistics, more and more students are seeking to take up the challenge of research that addresses social justice problems, and so, like in forensic psychology, the academic community is increasingly seeking experimental methods and alternative approaches to data collection or data generation. This chapter goes some way towards addressing this need by describing several different methods of language data collection that minimise the practical barriers and ethical risks usually involved in collecting data from human participants in the justice sector. These methods can be used for a range of student projects, but might also be scaled up to form the basis for major research projects or training programmes. Indeed, the origin of the first approach (section A below) was a police department training programme devised by leading psychologists in the field (Powell & Thomson, 1994).

Methods of data collection or generation

The data collection methods presented in this chapter cover a range of data types suitable for different types of analytical methods. The first example is a method for generating naturalistic spoken interview data with children, as mentioned above, but it could easily be adapted for use with adult populations. It uses a variation on the 'mock crime' experimental design, with participants first experiencing some staged event and later being interviewed about the details of the event. For those new to this field, there are several confounding factors to take into consideration when designing a mock crime (or in this case non-crime) event, but this design is effective and simple to implement for populations that regularly assemble as a group such as student groups or employee groups. Following the main description, there are some suggested alternatives for use with dispersed populations.

The second example is a more resource intensive method and was originally devised for a project that measured the performance of interpreters mediating communication in a police interview. Again, the data generated are spoken interview recordings; however the speech is not entirely naturalistic, as will be explained. This method is more appropriate for research that measures the performance of an intermediary such as an interpreter, legal counsel, cultural liaison officer or other third party support person.

The third example is a project for school-aged students that can be adapted to different year levels as required. It uses pre-generated texts and a simplified method of syntactically classified punctuation analysis to engage the students in an authorship attribution task. While its main function is to introduce linguistics into the classroom, a researcher could use the exercise to gather other kinds of data relating to the way that students perceive and approach language analysis tasks. This is an important topic given the role of language attitudes in shaping justice outcomes around the world and it will be discussed further in the final chapter of this volume.

The fourth method is drawn from sociolinguistics and can be used to gather real-world data in the justice sector through unobtrusive participant observation. This approach can be applied in public settings such as courtrooms that allow observation but not recording. This section also includes a brief mention of some further ideas for utilising publicly available data sources for linguistic research.

While this chapter presents several approaches to data collection or generation, it is not a comprehensive discussion of methodological theory. Rather, it is intended to recommend some practical solutions to the problem of data collection in the justice sector whilst maintaining the integrity of the linguistic analytic approach. There are, of course, many other aspects to research design to be taken into consideration, and any researcher that uses one of these methods will need to address the broader questions about methodology that are beyond the scope of this chapter. The focus in this chapter is on the relationship between the collection or generation of data and the linguistic analysis that is to be applied. For each of the approaches described below, methodological theory is only addressed to the extent that the broad requirements of the data analysis are met. So for example, section A addresses the requirement for naturally occurring spoken data in several forms of discourse analysis such as Conversation Analysis. It does not, however, discuss the relative merits of Conversation Analysis as a tool to investigate the linguistic features of a police interview (cf. Chapter 3). There are several more generalist books that address linguistic methodologies, some of which are listed in the references at the end of this chapter.

A. The VARE project

The Victoria Police Service in Australia trains police officers in the interviewing of children for the purposes of obtaining statements from witnesses and victims of crime. Since a change to the relevant legislation in the 1990s, the Video and Audio Recording of Evidence (VARE[3]) initiative has permitted video recordings of interviews to be used in place of a court appearance by a child during the presentation of the evidence in chief by the prosecution.[4] The main emphasis of the training course is the rehearsal of an interview technique that will elicit information in such a way that it can be used as reliable evidence in court. There are therefore certain parameters concerning both the type of information that is to be elicited and the way in which requests for information can be made. It is of primary importance that the information elicited is given freely by the child and without leading questions or verbal threats and bribes. Leading questions are defined by Powell and Thomson (1994) as those in which information is supplied by the interviewer as part of a question when the child has not yet given such information in the interview: '[l]eading questions imply the presence of information not previously mentioned by the child.' (1994, p. 209). For instance, the interviewer may not ask if *the man went home* when the child has not yet mentioned the gender of the person under discussion.

The VARE training course consists of theory and practical components and the interviewing skills of trainees are tested in a mock interview situation. In order to create the most realistic environment for these mock interviews, the VARE coordinators organise for groups of school children, aged about ten years, to attend interview sessions with the trainees. A few days prior to these interviews, the VARE coordinators arrange for the children's school day to be disrupted in some fashion. For example, two of the VARE coordination team might attend the children's classroom (in plain clothes) and pretend to conduct a survey of the children's afterschool activities. The disruption organised by the VARE coordinators is usually referred to as 'the Event' and it is used as a focus in the police-child interviews a few days later. None of the trainees are given any information about the Event before they interview the children, except that they are told the time and date on which the Event occurred and perhaps the type of class that it disrupted (e.g. normal class, assembly, special assembly, etc.). Each trainee officer interviews at least two children and they are given 15 minutes within which to complete the interview. The objective of the exercise is to use the skills taught in the training course to elicit as many details as possible from the child about the Event, including descriptions of the people involved. The interviews are video recorded and the recordings can be accessed later by the researcher without the need for any additional research staff to be present during the interview. Notably, the presence of the recording equipment does not imply any kind of observer paradox because the video camera would be present in a real investigative VARE interview. Any effect that the recording process might have on the participants in the training interviews would also occur in real interviews.

This very simple method can generate interview data that are naturalistic and unscripted, which is a great advantage over some of the other methods described below. Although the Event is contrived, it appears natural to the children and, importantly, children are not aware that the Event is connected to their trip to the police training facility. Heydon (1997) details the use of this method in an undergraduate research project and finds that despite the children being given consent forms and attending information sessions with their parents[5] about the trip to the police station, they did not realise that the disruption to their class several days prior to the trip was faked, nor that it was connected to the police centre excursion. This arrangement means that the interviews are conducted in much the same knowledge state as for interviews in a criminal investigation: the child does not know what they are going to be asked about, and the police interviewer does not know what the child has witnessed or experienced. As such, the method facilitates the creation of naturally occurring spoken data as required by Conversation Analysis and other forms of discourse analysis. The training interviews exhibit the same discourse features as a natural interview, including question-answer chains for next speaker selection, insert sequences, formulations, repairs and preference organisation. For instance, the method generates data that could be used to study the occurrence of a yes/no response to an indirect question that requested substantive information, e.g. Q. 'Do you know what he was wearing?' A. 'Yes.'

In using the Event to generate the topic of the subsequent interview, there can be confounding factors. For instance, sometimes the disruption organised by the VARE coordinators can co-occur with other disruptions to the children's usual school routine such as a special assembly which has to be arranged by the school staff in order to have all the children together for the VARE-related disruption. This co-occurrence can often cause confusion to the participants in the subsequent interviews, particularly if the interviewer asks the child a question like *Did anything unusual happen on Tuesday morning?* A question like this can often lead to the child giving a detailed narrative about the school-organised disruption and the interviewer may accept this as the target event to be discussed, not realising that s/he is on the wrong track.

Another potential problem with this method is that while it has the advantage of all the participants witnessing the same Event at the same time, if one member of the class or group guesses that the Event is staged, they might share this information with the rest of the group. In methods that expose witnesses to an Event individually (e.g. they each watch a video recording of a mock crime), there is less chance of this happening. However, the participant does not experience the Event in person and it is perhaps even more difficult to maintain the illusion that the Event was not staged for the purpose of the interview.

For police interview research involving children, the VARE method works well, and with the cooperation of the children's school and parents, it does not require expensive resources to execute properly.

B. Spoken data generation methods using scripts

For some types of research, it might be necessary to provide scripts to actors in a role-played interview to elicit spoken data from specific participant cohorts. One such doctoral project conducted at RMIT University in Melbourne, Australia by Ceyhan Kurt, a linguist and professional interpreter, uses scripts to investigate interpreter performance across modes (simultaneous and consecutive). The method devised by Kurt is based in part on recent work by Hale, Martschuk, Ozolins, and Stern (2017) and addresses the need to compare the performance of interpreters across controlled conditions of practice.

Kurt's model involves actors reading out scripts for the parts of the police interviewer and the suspect or witness, while the participant in the research (the 'subject') interprets between the actors. The performance of each interpreter can be measured and compared across the cohort, and variables of performance or interpreter quality (years of experience or training) can be manipulated as required.

The purpose of this approach is to achieve a controlled environment within which the interpreter's performance can be measured, whilst still applying as accurately as possible the conditions of a police interview. Research has demonstrated that the performance of the interpreter can be affected by emotive or psychological aspects of the interview such as the discussion of criminal matters, the use of swearing or taboo language and the heightened emotional state of the suspect or witness (Lai, Heydon, & Mulayim, 2015). Thus, in this method, attention is paid to the content of the scripts, using realistic crime scenarios and the generation of interview scripts requires considerable work to ensure that the actors' behaviour is as close as possible to a real police interview.

To achieve a realistic script, Kurt began with a published police interview transcript from an earlier research thesis. It would also be possible to use a police interview transcript that appears in records of a court trial or a publicly available police record of interview (these are published in the media from time to time). The original police interview was used to create a crime scenario and detailed backstory for the actors playing the police interviewer and the suspect or witness.[6] The actor playing the police interviewer was in fact a police detective, and this person was able to conduct the interview as though it were a real investigation using all the techniques and questioning patterns that he would normally use. Where the researcher is unable to obtain cooperation from a serving or retired police officer, the original police interview transcript can be used to generate questions and strategies for the actor to learn and apply in their role-play. The actor playing the suspect and witness was a Turkish language interpreter and used Turkish language exclusively in his role as a Turkish speaking interviewee. Both actors were required to study the notes provided about the two crime scenarios and their characters, just as they might for any performance. The actors were then filmed as they conducted the interviews from beginning to end as a sustained role-play. The interviews were mediated through an expert Turkish-English language interpreter.

This process resulted in video footage of two interviews conducted using natural language and with the details of each case based on real criminal investigations. All the legal processes that would normally be followed were played out such as advising the suspect of their rights and informing the suspect of the charges brought against them. Most importantly, the interviews included naturally occurring turn-taking, interruptions, repairs and turns of varying length.

The next phase of the data generation method was to create scripts from the material recorded by the actors. The naturalistic conversational patterns enabled the researcher to create highly realistic-sounding scripts for use in the actual laboratory research phase. Four scripts were created, one for the English language police role and one for the Turkish language interviewee role in each of the two interviews. The interviews were then conducted live using the scripts with role-players for the police and interviewee roles while the research participants, all Turkish language interpreters, performed the interpretation of the interview discourse. Each participant interpreted for two interviews, one with the suspect script and one with the witness script.

The laboratory was equipped with audio-visual recording equipment to capture the interviews and the resulting data were a set of English-Turkish interpretations of the same pair of interviews, with each participant interpreting once in the consecutive mode and once in the simultaneous mode. In this project, mode of interpreting was the main independent variable, but other variables could be investigated by changing the parameters of the transcripts (conditions).

This method does require considerable time to arrange and record role-played interviews for data generation and script-writing. However, it provides an accessible form of data collection for those working outside of the major forensic linguistics centres, or those without access to justice sector data. Only a minimal amount of authentic data is required to provide the role-players with realistic details and backstories and this can be gleaned from publicly available sources in most cases. Its main feature is that it can be used to conduct experimental research whilst maintaining aspects of ecological validity. By using scripts for the interviewer and the interviewee, many variables that might normally confound results, such as varying lengths of turn, can be controlled across multiple runs of the experiment. By creating the scripts from transcripts of actual interactions, many features of discourse in the justice sector can be maintained. The method can also be adapted to other forms of justice or legal interaction, such as a lawyer-client interview, a parole hearing or a courtroom cross examination. In addition, it is feasible to carry out the experiments with only basic audio-visual equipment, such as cameras and microphones, linked to a monitoring station in another room.

C. Data for classroom exercises in forensic linguistics

Linguistics has long been a standard part of English foreign language education in continental European universities but until recently, linguistics was rarely taught as part of an English language curriculum in English-speaking countries. 'English' as a school subject focused predominantly on fiction, creative writing and the classics, with some critical analysis of news and, occasionally, some grammatical or stylistic instruction. More recently, education boards in several English-speaking countries, including England, Australia and Singapore, have introduced alternatives to this traditional version of 'English' that cover linguistic concepts and analytic methods. These subjects such as English Language (in England and the state of Victoria, Australia) or English Language and Linguistics (in Singapore) introduce senior high school students to the analysis of language as a system, and the role of language in social and political life (see for instance Burridge & De Laps, 2015).

For those schools delivering the linguistics-based forms of English, or equivalent linguistic instruction in other languages, there is a dearth of materials to supplement the standard textbooks and almost no linguistic teaching resources available for junior high or primary school classrooms. Moreover, with a shift in focus to computer skills in early years school education (Wilensky, 2016), underlying skills such as syntactic analysis or parsing will support students to acquire computer programming competence. There is therefore a need to provide teachers with ideas and materials for linguistic instruction at an earlier stage than final year school certificate courses. This section presents a simple exercise that can be adapted for use with junior high or upper primary school students and does not require more than a basic knowledge of grammar, although some generalist linguistic preparatory reading, such as Crystal (2003), will enable a deeper engagement for students and teachers. The exercise can be combined with a statistical analysis of the results, thus incorporating a mathematical element, or a discussion of language variation and change for a social sciences focus. It can also be delivered as part of a philosophical discussion on reasoning and the nature of proof in a legal setting.

The exercise is based on a forensic linguistics case, similar to the authorship attribution case described in Chapter 1. The method was employed for a series of classes delivered at Auburn High School in Victoria, Australia for students in year 7 (aged around 12). It has also been adapted for use with upper primary students (aged 10–11). In the Auburn High School delivery, the teachers prepared sets of documents to be used by the students to solve a mock crime using a forensic linguistic analysis. The case involved the disappearance of the maths teacher, Mrs C, who had gone missing while on holiday in Greece. The main piece of evidence in the case was ransom letter allegedly sent by the kidnappers. The case revolved around the suspicion that the kidnapping was staged by Mrs C so that she could enjoy an extended break from her classes. To solve the case, the ransom note would be compared for authenticity with several emails that Mrs C wrote to her mother during her trip. For the sake of the exercise, the note was also compared to a second set of documents, which were several travel blogs written by the English teacher, Ms M.[7]

The method used for authorship attribution is the syntactically classified punctuation analysis developed by Chaski (2001, 2013). It has a known error rate of 14.2% (Chaski, 2013, pp. 15–16), which is too high for a real criminal court case, and Chaski has found that syntactically classified punctuation analysis is more effective when combined with other measures (Chaski, 2013), although the more complex method has limitations as well.[8] However, the classification and analysis of punctuation are manageable exercises for most students in the target age ranges, making this suitable for the classroom. The point of the comparison in this exercise was for students to determine whether it was more likely that the ransom note was written by Mrs C, or by another randomly selected person (Ms M). This is not necessary for the exercise to work, but it allowed for different teams to work with different data sets. More comparative authors can be added if desired, and, in fact, a larger pool of comparative texts would permit a 'line-up' of authors which might increase the reliability of the results (see below).

The students were provided with the case history, the suspicious ransom note and the two sets of documents (emails from Mrs C and blogs from Ms M). As a preparatory exercise, the students were asked to examine the documents and explain how they might carry out the task of authorship attribution. Students will often point to spelling errors or formatting patterns, which allows a discussion about statistical significance and the difference between a method based on valid scientific theories and a method based on stylistic comparison (see Chaski, 2001, 2013). Students were then introduced to syntactically classified punctuation analysis and taught how to identify and classify the punctuation in the documents.

Chaski (2001) establishes that the distribution patterns of punctuation can be used to differentiate between two texts written by the same author and two texts written by different authors. However, the punctuation patterns can only be used in this way if they are first classified according to their syntactic function, and then grouped into macro syntactic classes as described in the first step below.

Step 1. The anonymous text is analysed and each instance of punctuation is classified as belonging to one of five macro syntactic classes: sentential (sentence level eg the usual use of a full stop to end a sentence); clausal (clause level, eg the use of a comma to introduce a clause); phrasal (phrase level, eg the use of a comma to introduce a phrase); appositive (apposition and insertion level eg inverted commas used to denote an appositive or quote within the text); word-internal (punctuation within a word, eg an apostrophe denoting possession).

Step 2. The same analysis is performed on the comparison texts of known authorship

Step 3. The two sets of scores for the five syntactic categories are compared statistically, using a Chi Square 5×2 Contingency table.[9]

Step 4. The test establishes whether there is a significant difference between the two sets of scores. If there is a statistically significant difference, this indicates that the texts are more likely to have been produced by different authors. If there is no statistically significant difference, this indicates that the two texts are less likely to have been produced by the same author.

The analysis was carried out comparing the ransom note with the emails written by Mrs C and the results showed that there was no significant difference between the punctuation patterns in these two data sets. However, when the ransom note was tested against the punctuation patterns in Ms M's blogs, the test showed that there was also no significant difference. Thus, the testing found that the ransom note differed significantly from *neither* of the teachers and failed to discriminate between them as the author of the ransom note. Of course, this provided a valuable opportunity to teach the students about the importance of using valid tools for analysis. For those wishing to conduct more reliable experiments, Chaski (2013) presents a more sophisticated statistical analysis using a combination of measurements; however, the syntactically classified punctuation analysis is more accessible to most teachers and will provide many learning opportunities for students.

D. Sociolinguistic observational data collection

An alternative to using mock crimes or scripts to generate role-played data is to collect data from justice sectors where observation is permitted but recording is restricted. Courtroom or tribunal hearings are a typical example of this kind of setting. In many countries, courts are open to the public; however it is difficult or impossible to make electronic recordings of the proceedings. Even in those countries where some court proceedings are broadcast on television, such as the United

148 *Legal process*

States, the broadcast segments might not include the required data. For instance, the camera and sound might not pick up specific interactions of interest to the researcher. A number of studies have instead adapted the Labovian technique of collecting a narrowly defined data set to study just one or two sociolinguistic variables (Labov, 2006). This is a highly suitable method for undergraduate student projects or to supplement a broader analysis in a postgraduate research thesis or general research project. As in the Labovian department store experiments, it primarily involves narrowing the scope of the inquiry to an observable phenomenon that can be used as a reliable heuristic to answer the research question.

A study of questioning in the Refugee and Migration Review Tribunals (Findling & Heydon, 2016; Muniroh, Findling, & Heydon, 2018) used this observational technique to gather data on question types being produced by tribunal members during the hearings with visa applicants. Although the hearings are recorded, the researchers were unable to gain access to the recordings, but they were permitted to attend and observe hearings in progress. Researchers took into the hearing a prepared form which had a large table listing nine question types discussed in cognitive interviewing literature (see Chapter 3; Milne & Bull, 1999).[10] A second column had a space to make a check mark when any of the question types occurred. In this particular project, a second researcher took notes of the proceedings in as much detail as possible which added nuance to the findings on the frequency of the nine question types, but this is not essential for a small-scale project with a narrower focus.

A second example of this method is the study of conflicts between police and courtroom interpreter services by Gilbert (2014). Gilbert was interested in what happened when covertly recorded conversations in Vietnamese between alleged drug dealers are transcribed and translated by community interpreters into English for the police investigators and then rendered back into Vietnamese by court interpreters. He used the observational method in open court sessions to record instances of mistranslation and confusion in the communication between the Vietnamese-speaking witnesses and the court interpreter. These interactions were not captured by the court stenographer who only recorded the English language spoken in the trial. Gilbert, as a bilingual Vietnamese-English speaker, was able to follow the interactions in Vietnamese and note down each instance of miscommunication and clarification. Gilbert had also narrowed his observations to drug-related terminology, terms of address and pronouns, which he had identified through his research as the most problematic aspects of mistranslation in these types of trials.

One of the main differences between this type of data collection method and those described earlier in sections A and B is that, here, a great deal of more preparatory research is required before the data collection takes place. Deciding which variables are valid heuristics to answer the research questions can require many months of laborious desktop research and field interviews. However, once the data are collected, the analysis is fairly straightforward: the distribution patterns of a particular variable are counted and tabulated before moving onto the discussion of the findings. This needs to be taken into account in the planning stages of the research and for smaller scale projects, well-established measures need to be chosen. For example, the distribution of question types in an interview has been extensively researched as a valid measure of the quality of the interview as a whole (Griffiths & Milne, 2006) and so might be used by students for this type of research project.

In addition to traditional justice settings such as courts, police interview rooms and prison parole hearings, there is an almost infinite quantity of publicly available linguistic material on the internet. Some of this can be used for forensic linguistic research projects, although devising a suitable approach that enables voluntary consent to participate can still be a considerable hurdle. Reddit forums and Twitter feeds are perhaps the most commonly used sources for material based around a given topic. Facebook posts are very often not public and require the researcher to become a member of the community. Managing the membership of the group to ensure that everyone taking part has consented to be part of the project might prove tricky, and the age range of participants might be unknown.

If these issues can be managed appropriately, there are opportunities for a range of research projects involving online language in a legal setting. For example, forums where users discuss their experiences of sexual assault can be analysed using theories of narrative structure (Labov & Waletzky, 1997) or Halliday's Systemic Functional Linguistics (Halliday, Matthiessen, & Halliday, 2014) in order to understand more about how people disclose sensitive or taboo information. Large-scale analysis of online data, such as Twitter posts with a specific hashtag, can be used to identify changes in attitude towards a particular justice topic reflected in word use and association. Sociolinguistic analysis of discussion boards might be used to reveal patterns of engagement by different socially stratified groups. In addition to these written forms of language, the internet has a wealth of spoken data on platforms such as YouTube and through webinars and podcasts. Identifying a suitable forensic linguistic topic for research using these data might be challenging, but earlier we discussed one such study, which used the pleas for help in missing person cases as a data source for comparing deceptive and truthful spoken language. There are also many videos posted online which feature police arrests and other kinds of law-related interactions with the public. With all of these online sources, the quality and generalisability of the analysis will be limited by the extent to which the source can be authenticated. While the internet seems like an obvious source of written material for use in authorship attribution research, the researcher is inevitably limited by the anonymity of the online world. In short, we cannot say with absolute certainty who was actually behind the keyboard.

Conclusion

Despite the drawbacks to the various methods of data collection presented here, each of them has been used to produce high quality research findings in forensic linguistics. As set out in the Introduction, the need to involve a wider range of linguists in forensic and justice-themed research is pressing. Using methods such as these, forensic linguistic research topics can be explored by linguists and their students around the globe. By engaging with criminologists and lawyers, linguists in any university can begin to learn how language impacts on the lives of people involved in the justice system. Through this interdisciplinary cooperation, and using the suggested methods of data collection, high quality linguistic analysis can help reduce barriers to justice and create a fairer system for many under-represented and disenfranchised people around the world.

Notes

1. I refer here to those universities where there is a specialisation in forensic linguistics or where at least one senior academic in the field is supervising research students in relevant topics.
2. Ironically, some very extensive data sets have been collected in remote or developing nations, mainly because the ethical barriers to collection are low or non-existent. However, this is not a sustainable means by which forensic linguistic research may be advanced, in my view.
3. Formerly Video and Audio Taping of Evidence, or VATE.
4. The witness still appears in court, either live or via video link, for the cross examination.
5. Consent forms were completed by the children as well as their parents/caregivers and information about the research was provided verbally for the children that did not mention the Event in describing their participation. The written information sheets for the parents/caregivers described both the Event and the trip to the police facility, and parents had to agree not to disclose the connection between the two things to their children. Given the age of the children, it was not difficult to maintain the small subterfuge.
6. Kurt's research involved one script of an interview with a suspect and one with a witness, each relating to different crime scenarios.
7. Obviously this was a bit of poetic license, since the most useful comparison would be with texts written by the alleged kidnappers. Readers who plan to adapt this method for their classroom might devise a more realistic scenario to permit the pair-wise comparison of documents, such as the alleged kidnapper being identified in the note, and comparative texts authored by that person being found online.
8. For instance, the measure is only really capable of comparison between two potential authors at a time and the results will only identify the most likely author of those two candidates.
9. This is intended to be a simple statistical test for a classroom exercise and there are many factors which could be taken into account for more rigorous testing, especially given the small sample sizes. However, for the purpose of this exercise a free online tool can be used such as that available at Social Science Statistics (https://www.socscistatistics.com/Default.aspx).
10. Open-ended prompt; WH-question; yes/no question; why?; forced choice; multiple questions; leading questions; tag questions; statements.

References

Armistead, T. W. (2011). Detecting deception in written statements: The British Home Office study of scientific content analysis (SCAN). *Policing: An International Journal of Police Strategies & Management, 34*(4), 588–605.

Burridge, K., & De Laps, D. (2015). *Love the lingo: VCE English language units 1 and 2*. Healesville, Vic: Boobook Education.

Chaski, C. E. (2001). Empirical evaluations of language-based author identification techniques. *Forensic Linguistics, 8*, 1–65.
Chaski, C. E. (2013). Best practices and admissibility of forensic author identification. *Journal of Law and Policy, XXI*(2), 333–376.
Crystal, D. (2003). *The Cambridge encyclopedia of the English language.* Cambridge, UK: Press Syndicate of the University of Cambridge.
Findling, J., & Heydon, G. (2016). Questioning the evidence: A case for best-practice models of interviewing in the Refugee Review Tribunal. *Journal of Judicial Administration, 26*(1), 30.
Gilbert, D. (2014). *Electronic surveillance and systemic deficiencies in language capability: Implications for Australia's national security.* Doctor of Philosophy (PhD), Global, Urban and Social Studies, RMIT University.
Griffiths, A., & Milne, R. (2006). Will it all end in tiers? Police interviews with suspects in Britain. In T. Williamson (Ed.), *Investigative interviewing: Rights, research and regulation* (pp. 167–189). Cullompton, UK; Portland, OR: Willan.
Hale, S., Martschuk, N., Ozolins, U., & Stern, L. (2017). The effect of interpreting modes on witness credibility assessments. *Interpreting, 19*(1), 69–96.
Hale, S., & Napier, J. (2013). *Research methods in interpreting a practical resource.* London: Bloomsbury Academic.
Halliday, M. A. K., Matthiessen, C., & Halliday, M. (2014). *An introduction to functional grammar.* Oxon: Routledge.
Heydon, G. (1997). *Participation frameworks, discourse features and embedded requests in police V.A.T.E. interviews with children.* (Honours Thesis), Monash University, Melbourne.
Labov, W. (2006). *The social stratification of English in New York city.* New York: Cambridge University Press.
Labov, W., & Waletzky, J. (1997). Narrative analysis: Oral versions of personal experience *Journal of Narrative & Life History, 7*(1–4), 3–38.
Lai, M., Heydon, G., & Mulayim, S. (2015). Vicarious trauma among interpreters. *International Journal of Interpreter Education, 7*(1), 3–22.
Milne, R., & Bull, R. (1999). *Investigative interviewing: Psychology and practice.* Chichester; New York: Wiley.
Muniroh, R. D. D., Findling, J., & Heydon, G. (2018). What's in a question: A case for a culturally appropriate interviewing protocol in the Australian Refugee Review Tribunal. In I. Nick (Ed.), *Forensic linguistics, asylum seekers, refugees and immigrants.* (In press).
Powell, M., & Thomson, D. M. (1994). Children's eyewitness-memory research: Implications for practice. *Families in Society: The Journal of Contemporary Human Services, April*, 204–215.
Wilensky, U. (2016). Why schools need to introduce computing in all subjects. *The conversation.* Retrieved from http://theconversation.com/why-schools-need-to-introduce-computing-in-all-subjects-53793

Index

Aboriginal languages 7, 90, 136
access to justice 122, 128, 130, 132, 135, 145
account *see* narrative
adjacency pairs 47, 87; *see also* Conversation Analysis
admissibility of evidence 78, 79, 86, 89, 91
authorship attribution 2, 15–27, 140, 146–9; approaches to 16–17, 25; and computational linguistics 16, 17, 19, 20; and stylistics 16, 17, 20

behavioural analysis interview (BAI) *see* Reid method

charges, criminal 79, 82, 86–7, 144
civil law *see* legal systems
clarification sequence 47, 83–8, 90, 148
classroom projects 9, 81, 141, 145–7
coding data *see* qualitative data analysis
coercion *see* power, abuse of
cognitive interviewing 43–9, 50–4, 70, 99, 101–4, 113, 119–20, 148
cognitive load 62
common law *see* legal systems
common usage *see* reasonableness
confession 43, 45, 47, 53, 71, 73, 88
contamination of evidence 49, 51, 88, 98, 99, 102
contextualisation cue 87
Conversation Analysis 44, 81, 110, 111, 141–2
corpus linguistics 17, 20–4, 34
credibility assessment *see* lie detection
criminology 3, 7, 9, 65, 100, 105, 150
Criteria-based Content Analysis (CBCA) 61
critical discourse analysis 65–6
cross-cultural communication 112
customary law *see* legal systems

deception *see* lie detection
discrimination 1, 35–6, 128, 134, 136

ecological validity 62, 139–40, 145
education in linguistics 2, 6–9; for linguists 3; for school students 4, 145
ethics 5; and vicarious trauma 5
experimental research 61, 101, 104, 139–40, 145, 147–8
expert linguistic evidence 18, 25, 29, 34, 36, 90, 110; data quality in 22

field interviews 113–17, 127, 137, 148
formulations 81, 84, 142

Gricean maxims 48–9, 52, 84, 87, 101, 102, 122, 123

human rights 97, 128–30, 133–4, 137

institutional discourse *see* police institutional discourse
intended meaning 30–1, 35–7
interdisiplinary collaboration 4, 137
International Association of Forensic Linguists (IAFL) 5, 37, 78, 126; IAFL Code of Practice 5
interpreting and translating 2, 7–9, 79, 90, 112, 113, 123, 129–37
interrogation *see* Reid method
interruptions *see* turn-taking

judicial decision-making 2, 7, 30, 36–7, 111–13, 122, 132

language diversity 4, 127–37
language resources 4, 81, 85, 115, 129, 131, 134, 136
lawyers 7–8, 30, 37, 54, 78, 90, 132–4, 150

leading questions 113–14, 122, 141; *see also* question types
legal semiotics 30
legal systems 1, 7, 8, 97, 127–8, 133–4
legal terminology 86, 132–6, 148
legal texts 29, 31, 34–7, 79–83, 88–9
lie detection 1, 50, 53–4, 60–74, 124, 140
likelihood, in forensic reports 16–20, 24

miscarriages of justice 1, 2

narrative 33, 44–9, 51–3, 69, 73, 81, 98–106, 111, 114, 143, 149

observation methods 112–19, 121, 123, 141, 147–8
official languages 127, 134

participant roles *see* participation frameworks
participation frameworks 45–9, 53
PEACE model 41–3, 49, 60, 70–4, 98
plain English *see* plain language
plain language 79, 90, 136
Police and Criminal Evidence Act UK 41
police cautions 2, 3–4, 7, 41, 78–92
police institutional discourse 2–3, 41, 65–6, 80–7
police interviews 2, 4, 8, 41–55, 60–74; recording of 89; *see also* PEACE model; police cautions
police training 1, 41–3, 49–54, 60–1, 64–5, 67, 70–3
policy research 43, 66, 70, 127–9, 131, 137
polygraph 54, 63
post-colonialism 127–8, 137
power, abuse of 55, 70, 73, 78
pragmatics 8, 32, 35–6, 45, 49, 62–3, 101, 110–11, 122; *see also* Gricean maxims
punctuation 140, 146–7

qualitative data analysis 112, 116–17, 129
question-answer chain 47–8, 81, 84, 142
question types 45, 49, 51–3, 99, 100–1, 103–5, 113, 148–9

reasonableness 31, 34, 36
receipt markers 109, 110, 123
recontextualisation 80–1
Refugee Review Tribunal 8, 111, 148
Reid method 42–3, 50–5, 60, 70–4

school curricula for linguistics 4, 8, 140, 145–6
Scientific Content Analysis (SCAN) 1, 8, 61–74
self-administered interview 101, 107
semantics 2, 29–37
social media 25, 82, 97–8, 100, 149
sociolinguistics 41, 53, 64, 90, 110–11, 141, 147–9
syntactic analysis 31–3
syntax *see* syntactic analysis

telephone interviews 109, 113–14, 118–20, 123
therapeutic benefits of justice processes 98–9, 103–5
topic management 45, 47–53, 63, 81, 100, 110, 113, 143
turn-taking 4, 48, 49, 87, 101, 110, 144

Undeutsch hypothesis 61

Video and Audio Recording of Evidence (VARE) 141
voice identification 2

witness testimony 2, 7, 41, 50, 72, 97–8, 101–4, 131, 141, 148
written report interview protocols 99, 104